"This is not a how-to manual or a [ ] is 30 days of sweet truth drawn from the deep well of Scripture. Sarah and Linda repeatedly offer the water of life for the thirsty mom's soul. I found myself reading and rereading entries because of the robust grace they contain. This devotion will be a friend and a mentor to every mom who draws near."

Jen Oshman, Author; Podcaster; Women's Ministry Leader

"I loved this! Honest stories, practical help and big grace for real mums, from real mums. This book is like a chat and a cup of coffee with a loving friend. It's warm, honest, practical and filled with real-life stories that set us free from the burden of trying to be supermum by continually pointing us to God's generous grace."

Amy Smith, Podcast Host and Resource Writer, Faith in Kids

"Finding a good devotional book is harder than you think, and finding a thoughtful, hope-filled devotional for moms is even harder. That's why we are happy to commend these reflections. The writing is accessible, the stories are honest, and the gospel encouragement can be felt on every page. What a needed reminder for moms (and all of us) that God opposes the proud but gives grace to the humble."

Kevin and Trisha DeYoung, Christ Covenant Church,
Matthews, NC

"I wish I had had this devotional when my children were little! This will be a wonderful companion for every mom who has ever felt exasperated or exhausted in parenting and is looking for wisdom and encouragement—which truly is all of us. Sarah and Linda beautifully show us that God uses trials and weaknesses to mold us and our children, inspiring us to trust in God's endless grace."

Vaneetha Risner, Author, *Desperate for Hope* and
Walking through Fire

"*He Gives More Grace* is for every mom living in the daily delights and challenges of motherhood. This book is not a formula for parenting but a respite of joy, written from voices of experience. Sarah and her mom, Linda, know what it is to cling to God's grace—and they will show you how to do the same. If you wish you could have two wise and experienced friends come alongside you and lift your eyes to see more of the grace of God for you and for your children, this book is for you."

Courtney Doctor, Director of Women's Initiatives, The Gospel Coalition; Author, *From Garden to Glory*

"Linda's time-tested wisdom and Sarah's trial-tried perspective make reading this devotional feel like sitting down with trusted mentors. They somehow not only know exactly what you need to hear but deliver it in a way that is astonishingly relatable, easily digestible, practically applicable, and miraculously memorable (even for the overcrowded brain of this mom of little kids). It's not often that what feels like an easy read turns out to be a life-altering one, but that's what you'll find in this book: profound truths presented in a way that will make an immediate and beautiful impact on your motherhood journey."

Abbey Wedgeworth, Author, the Training Young Hearts kids' series

"At the heart of this book is a prayer and a poem. Need I say more? The short, simple chapters ooze grace and wisdom while being gritty and real about the complexities of parenting. I particularly appreciated the inclusion of discussing chronic illness and children with additional needs, and the value the authors placed on diversity of parenting styles and temperaments."

Linda Allcock, Author, *Deeper Still* and *Head, Heart, Hands* Bible notes

He Gives More Grace

SARAH WALTON | LINDA GREEN

thegoodbook
COMPANY

Linda

To my husband Ray and our children Michael, Stephen, and Sarah, whom God has used as instruments of his grace in my life.

Sarah

To my husband, Jeff. Thank you for faithfully standing by my side on the best and hardest of days.

And to my children, Ben, Hannah, Haley, and Eli— it's a true joy and privilege to be your mom. May you come to know the grace and forgiveness of Jesus Christ as your one and only true hope.

He Gives More Grace
© Sarah Walton / Linda Green, 2023.

Published by:
The Good Book Company

thegoodbook.com | thegoodbook.co.uk
thegoodbook.com.au | thegoodbook.co.nz | thegoodbook.co.in

Cover design by Jennifer Phelps | Design and art direction by André Parker

ISBN: 9781784989354 | Printed in India | JOB-007483

Contents

Foreword

There is a sign that hangs on the wall in our kitchen. It says, "Just Enough Grace for Today." Ours is a busy house, thanks to all that comes with raising four boys who, as I write these words, span the stages of childhood from toddlers to teenagers. Several times a week I find that sign cockeyed and hanging from a single nail, likely dislodged by a rambunctious child. It's a reality of my life as a mother but also, I think, a metaphor.

Few things expose our need for grace more profoundly than parenting. There's not a single one of us who thinks we're getting it right all the time. And... we're right. There are no perfect parents. While we might be comfortable with a margin of error in other endeavors, when it comes to raising our kids, the stakes simply seem too high. We've seen how a word spoken in anger can crush a tiny spirit. We've heard our children express their desire for more of our time and energy, and we've felt guilty when we couldn't give it to them. We've watched as our own sin patterns are passed down to the next generation. We've looked into the little faces that sit around our dining-room table and wished we could be the hero they need.

It's true: parenting provides ample reminders that we are finite and sinful; but, praise God, that's not the end of the story. Christian parenting is a master class in grace. When you fail your children, you need grace. When they fail you, they need grace.

God's word declares that where sin abounds, grace superabounds (Romans 5:20). In other words…

- where there are tantrums, there is abounding grace.

- where there is explosive anger, there is abounding grace.

- where there is selfishness, there is abounding grace.

- where there is bitterness, there is abounding grace.

The gospel means there is grace for every sin you and your child will ever commit. No wonder it's called the good news! Because of Jesus, our families need not be caught on the hamster wheel of fail, try harder, fail again. Instead, we can welcome the very real challenges of family life as opportunities to seek grace and to give it out.

Through the lens of grace, nothing is wasted. God uses your imperfect moments to draw your heart—and your child's—toward his perfect love. This is a paradigm worth flipping.

My own momma was a master grace-giver. I have a treasured memory of her lavishing grace on my oldest son, Eli. He was little—a bundle of blond hair and chunky arms and legs—but that didn't keep him from having BIG feelings. He was mid-meltdown and I was D-O-N-E dealing with the drama. (Been there? Done that?) I barked out a command and expected immediate compliance. Mom chose a grace-infused approach. She dropped to her knees and looked my little boy right in his big, blue eyes and she said, "Eli, I love you. Your momma loves you. Jesus loves you." She followed those simple words with a generous grandma hug.

There it was, on display for us all to see: grace. That was the moment I realized that grace is a gift we pass back and forth in our families. It was the tug that started to unravel my unrealistic notion that the best way to showcase the gospel to my children was by being a perfect parent. While I still hate my sin and the ways it puts shrapnel into the hearts of my children, I am also able to see that what God's word says is true (of course!). Where my sin wounds, grace heals. Where my selfishness separates, grace draws together. Where my parenting falls short, grace fills in the gaps. When my children sin, I seek to hand them the gift of grace. When I sin, they are learning to hand the gift back to me. Grace is the gift that keeps on giving. What a gorgeous gift it is!

Like my own momma did, in this book Linda and Sarah will drop down to eye-level and lovingly speak words of grace to you. As moms themselves, they know the challenges of parenting—but this is not a commiserating book. No, they will lovingly lift your eyes as you read through these pages. Not because they have parenting all figured out but because their identity is not primarily wrapped up in raising kids. They are first and foremost followers of Jesus, fiercely committed to knowing his word and applying it in the spilled-milk places of life. They are the wise friends you need for every heartache and hiccup of parenting. They will point you to the one who longs to lavish his grace on you and your family.

When it comes to parenting, I am fond of saying, "I'm a cracked pot, raising cracked pots." It's true! On our best day, we are nothing more than a family of sinners, desperate for grace. Though yours is a family of cracked pots too, you don't have to live enslaved to guilt. Instead run to the one who longs to lavish you with his grace (Ephesians 1:7-8). In him, your family is sure to find everything you long for. Even if it's just enough grace for today.

Eli, Noble, Judah, and Ezra's mom
(also known as Erin Davis)

LINDA GREEN has three grown children (including Sarah) and ten grandchildren. She's married to Ray and lives in Colorado. Linda served as women's ministry director at a large church in Chicago for 23 years.

SARAH WALTON is the author of several books including the award-winning *Hope When It Hurts*. She and her husband Jeff have four children and live in Colorado Springs. She blogs at setapart.net. Find her on instagram @sarahpwalton.

Introduction

Motherhood is one of life's most precious gifts and privileges. And motherhood is also hard.

Giving birth or adopting a child will fill your heart with an unimaginable love that has no end... and, at the same time, it can overwhelm you with the sheer weight of responsibility for the life you've been entrusted with. Motherhood will make you smile, laugh until you cry, and cry until you have no tears left (sometimes all in the same day!). It will make you proud and humble you. Just as you work out how to parent your kids, they'll grow and change, and you'll start working it out all over again. Some days will drag, but the years will fly.

There are a million (literally) "how-to" books on motherhood, to go along with no shortage of advice from parents, in-laws, friends, and women standing behind you in the line at the grocery store when your child starts whining.

We really don't want to add to all that. We just want to remind you, and reassure you, that whatever stage you're at, the thing you most need for the adventure of mothering is the thing you always have: grace.

It is God's grace—his abundant, overflowing, undeserved kindness—that is our greatest treasure even on the best days, and our anchor and hope also on the hardest ones. So this book is simply an invitation to embrace the grace that God purchased for you at the cross through the life, death, and resurrection of his Son, Jesus Christ. His grace cannot be earned; it can only be received by those who recognize their helplessness apart from Jesus. Like the nursing baby at our breast, the child who finds refuge on our lap, or the teen who pours out their fears late at night—when we run to, depend on, and cry out to our Father in heaven, he lavishes us with his all-sufficient, endless grace.

That's what we've both learned along the journey of motherhood—that grace makes all the difference.

LINDA'S STORY

I met my husband, Ray, on a blind date. Seven months later we were married; five weeks after that, we were unexpectedly transferred from the Chicago area to New Jersey, where I experienced one of the loneliest years of my life. One month before our first anniversary, after a difficult delivery, I gave birth to a son. Though my recovery was long, nothing could overshadow the joy of becoming a mom! After two years we moved back "home" and added another son and a daughter to our family. I loved everything about being a mom but, increasingly, fear of the "what if's" plagued me. What if something happened to my child? What if he rejected Christ? What if I failed to equip him to live in this world? It was as I read God's word in that season that I began to experience the peace and freedom of putting the full weight of my confidence in Christ.

I loved being the mother of boys, but I was also thankful when God blessed me with a daughter. I prayed that, one day, we would be close friends and sisters in Christ. So it was hard when, as a teenager, Sarah began to struggle with the pressures of a socially aggressive school culture and to rebel against us as her parents. Honestly, I was at a loss. I had just been hired by our church as co-director of the children's ministry, which ruled out homeschool options. We were unaware that she had contracted Lyme disease, which was taking a toll on her mental and physical health.

I can look back now and see that, behind the scenes, God was faithfully at work, answering prayers in ways we couldn't see at the time. In fact it was in what felt like our darkest night that Sarah, in a juvenile psychiatric hospital, surrendered her will and life to Christ.

As the last of our three children left home, I humbly marveled at God's grace through all the joys and sorrows of parenting. What I couldn't see then was how much I would need to continue to lean on God's grace in the season ahead. For when our first grandchild came along several years later, we entered what was to us the unfamiliar world of special needs.

In God's kindness, 45 years of marriage have blessed us with three children, two beautiful daughters-in-law, a faithful son-in-law, and ten precious grandchildren ranging from age two to 16. Two of our grandchildren have special needs, and all are a good gift from our loving Father. We love doing life with our loved ones, always praying that God will continue the good work of grace he has begun in each of us. This book is the fruit of that grace, reminding me that whatever comes, God gives more grace.

SARAH'S STORY

As much as it's truly a privilege to write this book alongside my own mother, our relationship hasn't always been sunshine and roses. As I navigated my middle-school and high-school years,

I spiraled downwards, often lashing out at the very one who loved, fought for, and sacrificed for me the most—my mom. But those years, though painful, didn't have the last word. The Lord brought me through that painful season and restored the relationship between my mom and me, which has blossomed into one of the relationships I cherish most today. Only a few years after the Lord set my feet on a new path, I met my husband, Jeff, and we've now been married for 19 years.

We've been blessed with four children, aged 16 and under. In many ways, motherhood has been far different than I expected, bringing both blessings and challenges beyond what I ever could have imagined. We've navigated special needs in one child, chronic illness in myself and all four children, financial woes and job loss, and countless challenges in between. And the story isn't yet finished. But mixed within all the difficulties, the years have also been filled with milestones, laughter, memories, celebrations, deep conversations, and countless lessons learned. Motherhood has truly been both the best and hardest thing I've ever done.

GRACE IN MOTHERHOOD

If you're picking up this book, we assume you're somewhere along the path of this wonderful, crazy, always-changing journey of motherhood. And we want one thing to be clear— we don't have all the answers! However, with over 60 years combined of navigating motherhood from infancy to adulthood, we have come to find God's grace to be a central theme throughout every season—and so it is the central theme of this book. Sister, whether you're in the throes of sleepless nights with an infant or navigating the complexities of the teen years or somewhere in between, we pray this book will meet you there in a tangible and practical way. We don't sugarcoat the realities of motherhood but enter into them honestly, because that is where God's grace meets us.

Because motherhood is as unpredictable as the weather, these 30 chapters are short and accessible, and you can read them in any order, on your own or with a group of other moms. And in each chapter we've summed it up in a single, short sentence—"Grace in a Line." Hopefully, you can carry that into your day and put it to use to point yourself to the love of Jesus as you seek to love your family.

And just to say, if you are reading this outside of North America, we appreciate that the way we abbreviate mother to "mom" looks odd to you. Thank you in advance for silently and graciously switching the "o" for a "u" every time you see it.

So curl up on your sofa with a cup of coffee or tea (or, if necessary, grab a few moments of solitude in the place moms often find to be the only place where they can find it—the bathroom) and let God's grace wash over you as you read the pages of this book. Wherever you find those few moments of quiet, we're grateful for the privilege of sharing in this journey of motherhood with you.

Whatever joys and sorrows, questions and insecurities, excitement and burdens you may be carrying today, know that you're not carrying them alone. You have a Savior who not only sees you but who knows exactly what you need to care for the children he's entrusted to you. Because, when all is said and done, you can be assured of this: he gives more grace (James 4:6).

With love,

Linda Sarah

Why Grace Is Such Good News

"And God is able to make all grace abound to you, so that
having all sufficiency in all things at all times, you may
abound in every good work."

2 CORINTHIANS 9:8

GRACE IN A LINE

I am God's beloved daughter, and he will
be enough for me today, all day.

A young mother recently asked me what I would say
to the younger version of myself if I had the chance.
Without hesitation I knew what I would say: "Don't
be so hard on yourself; God gives grace." She sighed and
replied, "How do you do that?"

Her question prompted me to think of how often I have
underestimated and failed to rely on the grace of God in my
parenting. Grace is one of those words Christians use all the
time, but it needs to be understood before we can start to
appreciate the gift that it is. Biblically, grace is God's favor
bestowed on undeserving sinners without any basis of merit.
God's gifts of spiritual and earthly blessings are all grace. We

have been saved by grace through faith in Jesus Christ, and we are being sanctified by grace through faith as well. Every breath we breathe comes through grace until we are in our eternal home, which itself will be a gift of grace. In the Christian life, everything is of grace.

GRACE APPLIED

When my kids were young, I knew God had saved me by grace apart from my own works; what I didn't understand was the importance of preaching grace to myself, kneading it into my life every day. Without realizing it, I was still living according to law: I was trying to please God and live his way by using my natural strengths and abilities to be a good wife, mother, and friend. But in all my striving and busyness, I was becoming overwhelmed with all the good things I was trying to do, until, one day, I collapsed on my bed and cried, "Lord, I can't do it all!" And in that moment God's grace was there to meet me as I sensed the Spirit whisper to my heart, I never asked you to.

God began to show me ways that I was focusing more on what I was doing for him than on what Jesus had accomplished for me! I didn't have to do it all because Jesus had done it all for me and continued to pour his grace out onto my life day by day. Of course we are called to do good works and to live holy lives, but we can only do that in a God-glorifying way by keeping the glorious truths of the gospel front and center in our lives. So I began to ask God to show me how I could experience the joy, freedom, and fruitfulness that were available by his grace.

God taught me first to remember that our salvation is in Christ (it's all about grace) and that the way we continue in the Christian life is to "work out our salvation" (Philippians 2:12). We are saved by grace, and we live by grace, "for it is God who works in you, both to will and to work for his good pleasure" (v 13). Even the power to obey God is through his Spirit—a gift, a grace. The same grace through which God saved us continues to flow to us each day in countless ways that bless us and show his benevolence towards us. God gives us gracious gifts of family and friends, provides for our needs, strengthens us in weakness, and equips us with all that we need for the work he calls us to do. From his good hand come gifts of laughter, tears, restful sleep, beautiful sunsets, restored health, protection, and comfort in our griefs. Everything we have been given is an undeserved grace from our generous Father.

The second thing we need to remember is that grace, not goodness, defines who we are. What's the first thing you think of when you read Ephesians 5:1: "Therefore be imitators of God, as beloved children"? Were you more struck by the command in that verse or the statement of your identity? Often our eyes fall on what we should do rather than on who we are: here, the staggering reminder that we have been chosen and adopted as God's beloved daughters. Take this in, sister. You are loved, and you are loved not because you are a perfect mom who is always patient with her children or keeps a spotless, organized home but because God set his affection upon you and chose you to be his daughter before the world was created, and sent his Son to redeem your life so that one day you can live forever in his presence. That is amazing grace.

This means that, when you have lost your temper and feel like a horrible mom, God draws near to you with tenderness and love. When you turn to him, he is quick to forgive you because your debt was fully paid by Jesus at the cross. Your Father sustains you in your weakness and is at work redeeming the moments when everything seems to have gone wrong. God's grace teaches us to run to him on our good days and our bad days, because he loves us.

So, whether you are fumbling your way through the exhausting newborn season with a colicky baby, attempting to patiently help a teenager navigate their wildly fluctuating emotions, or running children from activity to activity, this life-giving truth remains the same: "God is able to make all grace abound to you, so that having all sufficiency in all things at all times, you may abound in every good work" (2 Corinthians 9:8).

How do you experience God's grace each day? Here is my answer:

- Continue to grow in the knowledge and understanding of the grace Jesus purchased for you on the cross (2 Peter 3:18).

- Take hold of the truth that "sin will have no dominion over you, since you are not under law but under grace" (Romans 6:14).

- Set your mind on the hope and riches of God's glorious inheritance, to which we have been called, and "the immeasurable greatness of his power toward us who believe" in Christ's resurrection (Ephesians 1:18-20).

- Trust and rest in the finished work of God in Christ— read Hebrews 4:3.

- ~ Trust that God's sovereign plan is wiser and better than your plan (regardless of what a day might bring) because his plan is an eternal one—read Romans 8:28-29.

- ~ Keep watch for God's daily gifts of kindness, such as a friend taking your children for an hour or a day so that you can have some time to yourself, or the sun shining after a string of rainy days, or a child's snuggles on your lap. God's gifts of grace are all around us!

Being a mom who strives after a standard set by herself or others is exhausting. Instead, take long and frequent breaths of gospel grace, trusting that God is able to make all grace abound to you so that you may abound in every good work he calls you to for his glory. Because, after all and most of all, you are his beloved daughter.

REFLECT

- ~ Are there ways in which you struggle to apply the good news of God's grace in your motherhood?

- ~ What's one way you can rest in his grace today?

Journal

TWO

God's Good Gift — Your Kids

"Behold, children are a heritage from the LORD, *the fruit of the womb a reward. Like arrows in the hand of a warrior are the children of one's youth. Blessed is the man who fills his quiver with them!"*

PSALM 127:3-5

GRACE IN A LINE

My children really are a sign of God's
grace to me, every day.

Even as a little girl, I looked forward to being a mother and, in God's kindness, he blessed my husband and me with three children. I knew that each life entrusted to me as a mother was a gracious gift—a heritage and a blessing from God.

Yet the truth is that there were many days when it didn't really feel that way. There were days when part of me felt like turning in my badge of motherhood.

While memories fade over time, I clearly remember feeling like I would never feel rested again—ever! Trying to soothe a colicky baby who screamed for hours on end brought out emotions that unnerved me. The joy of motherhood was not uppermost in my mind whenever one of my children tracked mud all over the house, a teething toddler whined all day (and cried all night), or my four-year-old decided to give his little sister a haircut. Yes, there are certainly days when it is hard to see the little people in our midst as the gifts that they are. And, if you are parenting a child who has significant special needs, an extremely strong will, or mental or chronic physical illness, the burdens you feel may make it more challenging, at times, to appreciate the blessings.

Yet for every day, every child, and every situation, God provides abundant grace.

Someone wisely noted that the days of parenting are long but the years are short. From the vantage point of being a grandma, I heartily agree. The hard things felt very hard some days, but it's the countless memories of laughter, meaningful conversations, delight in a child's wonder, dandelion bouquets, and celebrations of growth that, woven together, have become our story and a testimony of God's faithfulness. Our challenge is to notice, enjoy, and celebrate in real time these moments with our children so that, when we look back decades later, we will be thankful that, by God's grace, we embraced each day to its fullest and enjoyed each of our children as the gift that they are.

However, looking back and looking around, I detect a couple of often unnoticed messages that undermine our ability to see our children as a blessing.

MAKING TOO MUCH OF THEM
This is the idea that as a mother, your life should revolve entirely around your children. Your kids should be the highest

priority and focus of your life. This sounds commendable—Christian, even. But if my kids are what is most important to me, then they have become an idol—something I love more than God and in whom I seek my sense of identity and purpose rather than in him. When children become little idols, we will find ourselves enslaved to their various demands and riding an emotional roller coaster that's determined by their ups and downs. When their happiness determines our own, we will tend to excuse things that should be disciplined, and when they have become our everything, we will be prone to hover over them and become overprotective parents.

Along with that, we will have unrealistic expectations of them. If my children are what gives me my sense of self-esteem, then I will need them to be successful. I will therefore tend to be too harsh on their mistakes, making me both quick to criticize and too quick to excuse. And a child that grows up thinking life revolves around them is heading for an abrupt awakening when they move out into the world and realize that it doesn't. When we make too much of our children, looking to them to give our lives meaning and fulfill our needs, we are setting both them and ourselves up for disappointment.

MAKING TOO LITTLE OF THEM
I have also witnessed well-intentioned moms (and dads) unwittingly putting other desires above the daily sacrifices that godly parenting requires, prioritizing seemingly more fulfilling worldly ambitions—be it career or comfort or something else. The dangers here are that children can feel neglected, that we miss precious milestones due to our absence or

distraction, and, ultimately, that we sacrifice a healthy relationship with our children altogether.

At which end of the spectrum do you fall?

While no mother ever plans to fall prey to one of these temptations, the truth is that, by nature, we all tend toward one or other of these errors. It is worth asking: which way does my own heart tend to lean?

I encourage you to take a minute before reading on. As you read of the ways in which we can be tempted, were you able to identify which error you are most naturally prone to? The good news is that when we recognize where our temptations lie, we can humbly seek the Lord's wisdom and help to overcome what might prove to be unhelpful to our children.

Thankfully, God's word tells us how to avoid both of these temptations. Jesus said, "Love the Lord your God with all your heart and with all your soul and with all your mind," and "Love your neighbor as yourself" (Matthew 22:37-39). While this is impossible in our own strength, the gospel gives us both the desire and power to live out this command.

When your first love is the Lord, you will be free to love your children in a way that reflects God's love for you in Christ, and you will see them as the gift that they truly are. Rather than making them the center of your world, you can parent them for their eternal good, even when it means saying no to something they want. With your focus on Christ, rather than seeing your children as a hindrance to other things you'd rather pursue, you can recognize the blessing that they are and the privilege you've been given of raising them up for the Lord.

The question is, how we can keep our focus on the gift that our children are when we're in the midst of mom exhaustion, toddler meltdowns in the grocery store, coping with children with physical or mental disabilities, fluctuating teenage emotions, or simply keeping growing children dressed and fed? What can help us find joy in parenting even during the most difficult days and trying seasons? It is by asking God to give us the right perspective: seeing that each child is a gift and each moment with them is a gift—even when it's hard.

- Look expectantly to God for the daily grace and wisdom that you need and that he has promised as you raise the children he's entrusted you with. This frees you to enjoy the privilege of teaching, training, and guiding your children to maturity, even when things don't go as you expect or would like.

- Marvel at God's delight in creating each of your children with gifts, abilities, and a unique personality and temperament to be discovered, nurtured, and used for his glory as they grow. Trust that it pleased him to choose you to be the mother of your children. On harder days, find help by asking the Lord to restore your perspective and joy. He is willing and able to renew a faint spirit, whether it's through a night of sleep, the encouragement of a friend, or reminders of truth from his word.

- Embrace and enjoy the season your children are currently in, with all of its challenges, uncertainties, delights, and blessings. The past is gone, and the future is uncertain, so practice being present today. Give yourself freedom and space to laugh at the craziness, dance in the kitchen, dig for worms in the mud with your child, take an unhurried walk with an exploring toddler, and bear with the ups and downs of teenage life. Above all, as you and your child delight together in the world they are discovering, seek every opportunity to point them to Jesus and their Creator.

Children are a heritage from God, given to us for a short season to love, enjoy, and proclaim gospel truth and grace to, until, we pray, we send them out as arrows to bear fruit for God's kingdom. And somewhere along the way, we come to understand that God's gift of children includes the blessing of God using them to make us more like Christ. They are a gift—a grace—not an idol or an inconvenience. There's joy for mothers who embrace this truth—even on (perhaps, especially on) the hardest of parenting days.

REFLECT

- Which way does your heart tend to lean—toward making too much of your children or too little of them?

- Even if you're in a difficult season, in what three ways can you see your children as a gift of God's grace?

Journal

THREE

The Beauty of Christ's Strength in Our Weakness

"[God's] delight is not in the strength of the horse, nor his pleasure in the legs of a man, but the LORD takes pleasure in those who fear him, in those who hope in his steadfast love."

PSALM 147:10-11

GRACE IN A LINE

It's okay to be weak; my kids most need a mom who loves Jesus, not one who has it all together all the time.

Motherhood is often beautiful and filled with countless moments of joy. Yet motherhood also contains moments, days, and seasons that are difficult and painful. There have been times when I've looked at my children and felt overwhelmed by the weight of the responsibility of raising them, given the obstacles we've faced. Living with chronic illness makes motherhood physically painful, and having passed that illness on to my four children is emotionally painful.

Sarah Walton and Linda Green

I have the desire to bring up godly, well-balanced children, yet I often feel as though I never get beyond simply keeping bellies full, preventing World War III from breaking out in our home, and getting through the day—all while carrying a thousand-pound backpack filled with fears, doubts, grief, and weariness.

Oh, how different life is from the naive picture that I had formed in my head before the realities of motherhood began. Don't get me wrong, I am thankful to be a mother. It is a precious gift and privilege. However, for better or worse, it's also a journey that's been far from what I imagined. And maybe you can relate.

A MOM'S INTERNAL STRUGGLE

I'm failing to be the mom that my kids need.
Will they always carry the baggage of the pain they have faced?
The burdensome trials in front of me are too much to bear.
If only I had done more.

Each mother carries her own unique fears, anxieties, and struggles, but all of us desire to be the mom that our children need. It's that desire that, combined with a sense of our own weaknesses, triggers our inner monologue. And that monologue will either consume us and create perpetual anxiety within us or it will lead us to the one who is not only in control but knows exactly what our children need—and loves them more than we ever could.

WHAT YOUR CHILDREN NEED MOST

If you are feeling overwhelmed, inadequate, or discouraged as a mom today, join me in reminding yourself of the God we serve and viewing your role as a mother through the lens of what he says in Psalm 147:10–11:

> *"His delight is not in the strength of the horse, nor his pleasure in the legs of a man, but the LORD takes pleasure in those who fear him, in those who hope in his steadfast love."*

God offers you something far better than a "try harder, be better, do more" mentality. God isn't expecting you to get every parenting decision right or to know and be all that your kids need. More than anything, he desires a heart that fears and submits to him as Creator, King, Savior and Lord, and trusts him as our heavenly Father, whose unending love flows from each facet of his character.

God's delight is simply in "those who fear him"—which means to see ourselves in light of his power, holiness, sovereignty, love, and sacrifice. Unlike a child who only obeys because they're afraid of what their mother or father may do to them if they do not, God desires us to follow, obey, and draw near because we know that we are safest, strongest, and most satisfied when we find our hope in him and his promises. In other words, he wants us to live by faith. He does not want you to think you are strong and therefore be self-reliant, but to know that you are not strong and therefore trust him.

So, although there are many good things we can offer our children, before all else, our children need these three traits in their mom.

1. A MOM WHO LOVES JESUS MORE THAN ONE WHO "DOES EVERYTHING RIGHT"

We will fail our children at times. We will overreact, overprotect, waste our time, pass on a bad habit, discipline in anger, or neglect to discipline. We will make mistakes, and sin will be intermingled with even our best efforts. So trying to be the perfect mother for your children will always leave you discouraged, guilt-ridden, and weary. Your children need you to stop fixating on your successes and failures and to fix your gaze on Christ.

We do this by shaping our lives with his word and making focused time with him a priority. Though this will look different in different seasons, we do need to make time to bring our weary and striving selves to the truth of his word and allow the Spirit to fill us with more of Jesus.

If you always get it right (or make it look as though you have), your kids will never see the preciousness of grace in your life. When you get it wrong, and repent and embrace forgiveness, they see what grace looks like lived out. You will still fail, yes, but as you seek to know Christ in tangible rhythms of life, you will grow to love him more—and that love will naturally overflow into the lives of the precious children who are watching you.

2. A MOM WHO TRUSTS GOD'S PLAN, EVEN WHEN IT'S NOT HER OWN

My experience as a mother has been nothing like I'd expected. Special needs, chronic illness, doctor appointments, physical limitations, and financial loss were not in the plan. I admit that I have resisted humbling myself and accepting God's path for me and my family on numerous occasions. During those times, I have found myself quick to give into irritation, self-pity, and loneliness because I've been fixated on what I wish life would be, rather than surrendering and humbling myself under God's good plan for me and my children (in other words, fearing God).

But through these hard years, I have learned that humbling myself under God's plan leads to joy. Jesus' path led to life through the cross, and he has told his followers that it will be the same for us (Matthew 16:24). This does not mean that I will always walk around with a smile on my face despite the difficult realities at hand. It does mean that by faith I choose to bring my heartache, disappointment, and weariness to Jesus, asking him to help me trust his goodness and purposes in my circumstances.

When your plans don't work out, and you pray through that with your kids, audibly saying to God, "Not my will but yours be done," you are showing your kids that God's ways are best, even when you can't see how.

3. A MOM WHO KNOWS GOD IS BIGGER THAN OUR BAGGAGE OR FAILURES

It's easy to look at the circumstances that you or your children are facing and feel defeated and overwhelmed. We will all be faced with circumstances that are far beyond what we can handle by ourselves.

However, the blessing of facing these unchosen circumstances is that they provide an opportunity for us to let go of our need for control and our desire to earn God's acceptance, and instead to trust that God is greater than the most hopeless circumstance and rebellious heart. Life's trials can become turning points that transform us from being moms who strive for control and perfection into moms who confidently trust in God's forgiveness, faithfulness, and redemption.

What a powerful witness it is to your children when they see peace and joy flowing from their mom amid challenging circumstances. What greater gift can we give our children than to give them a glimpse of our trustworthy Savior, who is greater than our sin and greater than our trials?

IN HIS STRENGTH

Sister, if you find yourself facing circumstances that are more than you can handle, or you feel inadequate to be the mom you desire to be, remember that the Lord's delight is not in strength or ability but in "those who fear him, in those who hope in his steadfast love." As you learn to trust Christ, rather than your own wisdom and strength, and as you learn to hope in God's steadfast love, rather than be consumed by your own failures or shortcomings, he will guide, equip, and strengthen you to be the mother he desires you to be.

REFLECT

- ~ In what ways do you feel a sense of weakness as a mom?

- ~ How do these three traits offer hope in your weakness, and what would it look like to rest in God's strength instead of your own today?

Journal

FOUR

It's Not All Up to You

"For by grace you have been saved through faith. And this is not your own doing; it is the gift of God."

EPHESIANS 2:8

GRACE IN A LINE

My children's salvation isn't up to me; it's up to God. I may not get every decision right, but God's grace is greater than both my successes and failures as a mom.

Whether you've been a mom for 40 days or 40 years, I'm sure there have been moments when you question whether you made the right call or you regret the way you handled a situation. You may even carry the burden of feeling that some of the decisions you made have contributed to problems that followed. Maybe you're facing a decision right now and feeling unequipped to handle that.

Let me assure you that every mom has been there or will be eventually. How do I know this? Because motherhood is made up of one decision after another. Which diapers do I use? Should I bottle feed or breastfeed? Should I sign them up for this activity? Should I work in a job or stay home with the kids? Is this a good friend for them to spend time with? Is public (state) or private school, or homeschool best for my child? Should I let them have sleepovers? Is this television show or book series appropriate? How do I best respond to their behavior or attitude right now? Do I give them a phone at this age when all their friends have one? Should I let them ride their bike to the store by themselves? Should I let them date yet? The list could go on and on.

And if you've been a mom for any time at all, you quickly realize that most decisions aren't black-and-white. You and a close friend may both be parents who desire to raise their kids in the truth of God's word, and yet you each come to different conclusions as to how that looks in some of these areas. Though we may have the best of intentions, we'll sometimes make a decision that we'll later wish we hadn't. And more often, we'll make a decision and never know whether it was the best one. So we can constantly be looking around and wondering, "Did I make the right choice? Should I have handled that differently? If only I had known better at the time."

I know all too well that these thoughts can quickly become all-consuming and paralyzing for a parent. When I think back to my years as a first-time mom, a wave of sadness sometimes washes over me. I wish I had known the challenges my child was dealing with at the time. I would have responded differently to so many situations had I understood the limitations he had from his unseen illness. If only I had known then what I know now, maybe things wouldn't have gotten as bad as they did.

But the Lord has met me in this place of insecurity and questioning with the truth that this guilt-ridden thought process is rooted in the assumption that I should be as all-knowing as God is. But the truth is that we can only see what's right in front of us. God doesn't ask us to foresee the outcome of every decision, and the outcomes of our children's lives are not solely dependent on each of those decisions. In reality, we can think we've made the best parenting choices possible, and our child still ends up walking away from the Lord and making choices we're saddened by. Or we may feel that we've really messed up, and yet our child matures and does well, and we discover that some of our poor choices actually ended up leading that child to see their need for a Savior.

The point is this: God doesn't give us eyes to see the future; he simply gives us the moment at hand and asks us to depend on his guidance, wisdom, and grace, one step at a time.

HIS GRACE COVERS OUR SUCCESSES AND FAILURES

I didn't know my child was dealing with misunderstood special-needs challenges when he was little. This meant that our attempts to guide, discipline, and teach him often backfired and left us with great confusion and a deepening sense of failure.

But that season also brought me to my knees and showed me that I needed God's help in that moment, one step at a time. From my limited human viewpoint, I couldn't see what lay ahead or even understand the moment at hand, so I learned to pray for wisdom and guidance, and then I did what I thought was best with what I could discern. Was it always the best choice? No, probably not. But that's okay—

because even though our choices in this life carry consequences, God's grace and sovereignty carry far more weight.

We see this clearly in the account of Joseph. When he was a boy, his father, Jacob, decided to show him favoritism over his brothers. His brothers responded by selling him into slavery out of hatred and jealousy. I think it's safe to say that the choices of his father and brothers had adverse consequences. But despite what the brothers had meant for evil, God was at work. He used their foolish and wicked choices to accomplish his perfect will. He rescued Joseph, and, as a result of that, he rescued the whole family as a result.

We serve the same unchanging redeeming God. Our choices do have consequences—yet even our worst parenting moments can't thwart God's will for our life or our children's lives. That is God's amazing grace.

Sister, God doesn't expect you to get every parenting moment right, and he doesn't need you to. Praise God that our children's future and salvation aren't solely up to us! The knowledge that God is the one who saves, and not us, is liberating when we face a parenting decision or regret a previous one, because their ultimate future doesn't hang on us getting it "right." It's humbling, too, and should bring us to our knees because what we should most want for our children we cannot do ourselves. So we plead with him to use our parenting—the parts we get right and the parts we don't—to bring them to faith or to build up their faith. It's not up to you, mom—so be released from that burden and lift your kids up in prayer to the one it is up to. He calls us to be prayerful, not all-knowing.

So now, when I look back at moments that I wish I had handled differently, I can resist the urge to beat myself up.

Instead, I can rest in God's grace and thank him that he can use even my flawed parenting to bring about his redeeming purposes in my life and, I pray, in the lives of my children.

And so can you.

REFLECT

- ~ Can you think of men and women in the Bible who made foolish choices as parents but saw God's grace at work in spite of those failures to bring about his good and perfect will for their child?

- ~ What burdens or decisions are you carrying today that you ought to lay before Christ so that you can choose to trust his faithfulness over your own success or perceived failings?

Journal

FIVE

Worship in the Mundane

"If I, then, your Lord and Teacher, have washed your feet,
you also ought to wash one another's feet ... If you know these
things, blessed are you if you do them."

JOHN 13:14, 17

GRACE IN A LINE

God will see and use every mundane act of service
that I do today.

From God's perspective, the extraordinary often comes wrapped in very ordinary moments and days.

One thing common to every mom's life is the many mundane duties repeated every week or every day. Clean laundry, folded and put away, is undone by the end of the same day as dirty clothes are tossed into the hamper (or on the floor next to the hamper!). Meals that require planning, shopping, preparing, and cooking are no sooner eaten than someone has opened the refrigerator looking for something more to eat. Kitchen counters seem endlessly cluttered with half-drunk water bottles, crumbs, and school papers. And as the kids get older, we can often feel reduced to nothing more than a chauffeur taking children from point A to point B.

The daily duties of caring for the needs of our family can often tempt us to feel discouraged and hindered from doing "more meaningful work." Do you ever compare your days now with the job you used to do, the travel you used to go on, or the ministry you enjoyed before you had children, and feel that your "mom world" is small and constrictive? Yes, being a mom brings countless joys, but the reality is that many of our days can feel unexciting and ordinary!

Over the years, I have come to understand that from God's perspective, the extraordinary often comes wrapped in very ordinary moments and days. The challenge is to share his perspective! How can routine household duties and time spent serving family members (who may, or may not, be grateful) be something we see as a gift to us, not a burden placed upon us?

Here are six practical ways in which you can use what might seem like merely ordinary moments as reminders that, with God, the things we often mindlessly (and sometimes begrudgingly) do can become extraordinary opportunities to give thanks and worship the Lord and bring joy to ourselves.

1. BLESS THE LORD FOR WHO HE IS AND WHAT HE HAS DONE FOR YOU

"Bless the LORD, O my soul, and forget not all his benefits." (Psalm 103:2)

The psalmist helps us lift our eyes to the Lord by giving weary moms a song to sing as we change diapers, get up in the early hours to care for sick children, or prepare dinner while toddlers (or teens) demand our attention. No matter how unglamorous your life may feel at times, God is pouring out his mercies upon you—some seen, many more unseen. Rehearse his extraordinary benefits to you. (To help you do so, you could seek to memorize the rest of Psalm 103.) When you view each moment in the eternal light of God's many mercies to you, you will always have a song of praise to sing.

2. COUNT YOUR BLESSINGS

"A faithful person will be richly blessed."
(Proverbs 28:20, NIV)

Ordinary moments in life can serve as reminders of the countless blessings we have been given. Dirty socks have housed the feet of the children we love, while dirty dishes can remind us of God's abundant provision of our daily needs. Sunrises can take our breath away when a tiny cry wakes us before dawn. As you take time to appreciate all you've been given, your hearts will start to fill up with thanksgiving.

3. REMEMBER THE GOSPEL

"Continue in the faith, stable and steadfast, not shifting from the hope of the gospel that you heard."
(Colossians 1:23)

Nothing will lift our eyes to the Lord and reorient our hearts more than remembering that, while we deserve God's wrath for our sin, we have been given a certain hope of eternal life through Jesus Christ.

It's natural for us to focus on what's hard, overwhelming, or weighty in our lives. Most of us find it harder to fix our thoughts on Jesus. Away from the noise of the world, daily routines can become moments to reorient our hearts to God's promises, which will ultimately lead to true and lasting joy. My encouragement to you is this: speak the gospel aloud to yourself every day. As the truth of who you are as an adopted daughter of the King of glory freshly works itself into your soul, you will be spurred to serve him, even when his eyes are the only ones that see what you do.

4. GIVE THANKS FOR THE PRIVILEGE OF SERVING LIKE JESUS

"Even … the Son of Man came not to be served but to serve, and to give his life as a ransom for many."
(Matthew 20:28)

Motherhood provides daily opportunities to be like Jesus in our humble acts of service. The paradox of the gospel is that to be low is to be high—to die to self is to find resurrection life. Jesus washed his disciples' feet and stretched his arms out on the cross to serve you. In the same spirit, each hidden act of service can become an altar upon which you offer yourself as a living sacrifice to the Lord. As you serve in the way he does, you worship him and discover that it is blessed to be like him (Romans 12:1; John 13:17).

5. REMEMBER THAT GOD SEES EVERY SECRET SACRIFICE

"Your Father who sees in secret will reward you."
(Matthew 6:4)

Jesus warned his disciples (and us) against doing what is right in public in order to be seen and praised by others. Rather, he says, we are to give to those in need quietly, not looking for praise or reward from this world.

Motherhood provides many opportunities to serve "in secret." God sees. He sees how much you long for a night's sleep but you still get up when a young voice cries out in the night. He sees when you set aside time to build with Legos or play dolls with a young child when you would rather be doing something else. He sees when you go without something you would love to buy so that your children can enjoy a trip out or a new toy.

The truth is that every "cup of cold water" given in the name of Christ will one day be rewarded (Matthew 10:42). There is no act of love or sacrifice offered that goes unseen by your heavenly Father. While wiping runny noses, vacuuming up dog hair, patiently repeating instructions to a distracted or disobedient child, and other unglamorous aspects of a mom's life may seem unlikely acts of worship, you can trust that, in God's eyes, he sees, and he smiles, and he speaks a "Well done, good and faithful servant" over your labors.

6. PRAY GOD'S WORD FOR THOSE YOU LOVE

"Continue steadfastly in prayer, being watchful in it with thanksgiving." (Colossians 4:2)

A wonderful way to love family members is by using the space and time that mundane tasks offer us to pray according to God's will as revealed through his word. This means the washing machine, the seat of your car or the chair at your desk can all become altars upon which you offer up prayers on behalf of those you love.

When hidden acts of service are offered as acts of worship, God grants us the privilege of using ordinary days to impact eternal realities. And in these common yet sacred moments, the ordinary becomes extraordinary—because God is glorified and we experience the blessing of work done for others, in his sight.

As you finish reading, look back through our list. Ask God to help you begin incorporating two of these principles into your daily routine this month. As they become habits, choose another two to focus on—until the ordinary and mundane things of mothering, while still not glamorous, have been transformed into extraordinary moments of worship, filled with the inexpressible joy of the Lord.

REFLECT

- ~ What are some typical "mundane" things that are part of your life in your current season? Invite God to open your eyes to see how you can use what feels ordinary and unappreciated as an opportunity to worship him.

- ~ Which one or two things from this list will you try to put into practice this week?

Journal

SIX

When You're Out of Your Depth...

"If any of you lacks wisdom, you should ask God, who gives generously to all without finding fault, and it will be given to you."

JAMES 1:5 (NIV)

GRACE IN A LINE

God will give me wisdom to parent well in every situation—I just need to ask.

*B*elieve it or not, my children don't always get along. As much as they are the sweetest of friends at times, they also push each other's buttons, measure the size of their cookie in comparison to their siblings', and hurt each other's feelings. At times, the issue at hand is fairly black-and-white, but often I find myself facing a conflict or decision that is a shade of gray. In those moments, it's easy to feel paralyzed with uncertainty and therefore not really deal with the situation at all, or react out of emotion and make speedy assumptions about what has happened, only to regret my hasty and unhelpful response a little while later. And it's in those moments that I've come face to face with my shortcomings as a mom, because I don't know what to do, and I don't have the answers, and I lack the ability to work out who really said what to whom, in what order, and why.

Those moments increase my sense of inadequacy. And yet they are also a gift (albeit one I don't often see as a gift at that time) because they lead me to see my utter need for the Lord's guidance and wisdom in a practical, moment-by-moment way.

REFLECTING BEFORE REACTING

One of our children tends to feel her feelings very deeply. She's a passionate, funny, and sensitive little girl. But when she makes a mistake, sins, or feels embarrassed, those strong emotions swing from one extreme to another within nanoseconds. And in those moments, I sometimes feel paralyzed as her emotional volcano erupts in front of me. At other times, I wrongfully erupt right back.

But God has been gently prodding me in those moments to take a deep breath, stop, and pray before I react. I may not know how best to respond in these moments, but I have a perfect Father who does. And God tells us, "If any of you lacks wisdom, you should ask God, who gives generously to all without finding fault, and it will be given to you."

When we feel our lack, we have this incredible promise. God will be faithful to give us the wisdom that we need in these moments—if we ask. This means that, having asked him for wisdom, we can proceed with a conversation or decision, knowing that God is guiding us into what is wisest, even if it doesn't feel like that or we can't see him doing it.

And I have seen him be faithful in doing so time and time again.

CALLING OUT FOR WISDOM

Recently, one of these conflicts occurred between two of my children, landing me in one of those difficult "gray areas." As I tried to step in to calm the situation, my daughter (who had been the one at fault) erupted in tears with a louder scream than her little body should be capable of and ran upstairs in anger. As my brain tried to catch up with the speed of her emotions, I couldn't make sense of her reaction when she was the guilty party in the conflict.

After a few minutes, I joined her at the top of the stairs, feeling at a loss for words and unsure of how to get to the bottom of why she so often erupted and ran away when problems blew up—even those she caused.

As I sat next to her, trying to keep control of my own emotions, I silently prayed, "Lord, help me! I don't understand her right now, and I don't know how to handle this. Please give me patience and wisdom. Please help me help my daughter with her overwhelming feelings."

I put my arm around her and just held her for a moment. As I did, a realization suddenly became clear. Her anger, tears, and seemingly impenetrable wall of emotion were rooted in something entirely different than I had first assumed.

At the root of it all was shame.

My sweet daughter was overcome with embarrassment, and ultimately shame, because she knew she had done something wrong. And in that shame, she wanted to run and hide, pushing away everyone around her.

My heart started to soften toward her, and I felt a wave of compassion because I know that struggle all too well. In the face of my own sin, I've seen the temptation to hide it, run from it, or put the blame on someone or something else. My little girl's sensitive spirit was overwhelmed by the embarrassment and shame over the ugliness of the sin that had just come out of her, and she felt trapped in its grip.

In that moment, the Lord gave me the insight to ask questions that helped her make sense of what she was feeling. I then shared how I also struggle with feeling embarrassed and ashamed when I do something that I know is sinful, especially when I hurt those I love in the process. I asked her if she felt sad that she had hurt her sibling, and she nodded through her sobs. So I shared with her that we feel shame because we're faced with the reality that we fall short of God's holiness. And we naturally want to hide from it, like Adam and Eve in the Garden of Eden. But that feeling of shame is meant to point us to Jesus, our Savior, who's always ready to receive us with his love and forgiveness.

I shared with her that when we feel shame over sin, we have two choices. We can either let it consume us or we can go to Jesus, say we're sorry, and ask for his forgiveness. Then we can go to the person we hurt and ask for their forgiveness. We always have a choice, but we need Jesus' help to make the right one.

God's grace to me in that moment was to give me the wisdom I needed but did not have, which led to an unexpected quieting of her emotions and a sweet conversation that allowed me to share with her the good news of the gospel in a fresh way. Did it keep her from ever responding that way again? Definitely not! But it planted seeds of truth that will in time, Lord willing, teach her to bring her strong emotions and feelings of shame to Jesus in repentance, rather than allowing them to consume her.

THE STUDENT AND THE TEACHER

As we sat at the top of the stairs, God was teaching me just as much as I was teaching my daughter. And he was faithful in answering my cry for help in the process.

Consider for a moment how you tend to respond when you're not sure what to do with your kids in a particular situation, or when a decision seems unclear. Do you panic? Do you avoid doing anything? Do you dive right in and try to figure things out as you go? All these are natural reactions as you come to moments when you simply don't know what to do. But the grace of God is to give wisdom when we ask. So next time, stop and take a deep breath. Don't run away. Don't jump to conclusions. Call on the Lord for wisdom and then trust that his Spirit is leading you in what you ask and say and do next.

Sister, you're not left to your own resources to navigate the complexities of motherhood. If you are a child of God, you have the Holy Spirit, our Helper, in every single moment you face in life. Instead of simply reacting, you can literally or figuratively fall on your knees and ask for wisdom and guidance. For "the purposes of a person's heart are deep waters, but one who has insight draws them out" (Proverbs 20:5, NIV).

May the Lord grant you the insight to do just that as you depend on him to raise these precious children that he has entrusted to you. And as you do, you just might see your own heart changed in the process.

REFLECT

- ~ How do you typically respond when you feel inadequate or unsure of how to handle a parenting situation?

- ~ What specific circumstance do you need to bring before the Lord and ask for his wisdom and guidance?

Journal

SEVEN

You're Only Human (and That's Okay)

"For he knows our frame;
he remembers that we are dust."

PSALM 103:14

GRACE IN A LINE

Jesus is not asking me to do anything I can't do,
and he'll help me with all that he does ask me to do.

I'm guessing that I'm not the only mom who has felt overwhelmed by all the things I need to do, others expect me to do, I believe others expect me to do, and I expect of myself! At times, when the accumulation of expectations threatens to crush me, I cry out, "I'm only human!"

While motherhood and raising a family brings great joy and countless blessings, the responsibilities that come with it can also, at times, make us feel overwhelmed, fearful, and uncertain. Let me ask you:

- Do you sometimes feel like the weight of the world (such as your children's salvation) is on your shoulders?

- Do you feel like you can never please everyone?

- Do you go to bed at night feeling guilty or frustrated by what you never got to, rather than grateful for God's mercies that day?

- Do you tend to measure your worth by what you have accomplished in a given day or week or year?

- Do you sometimes escape into social media just to get some moments of relief from the relentlessness?

If you're like me, I imagine you could answer yes to one or more of those questions, and sometimes all of them at the same time!

The good news is not so much that every mom wrestles with this one way or another, but that, amazingly, Jesus himself knows what it's like to live in a body limited by time and space in a sinful world. The Creator, who made man out of dust, himself became a creature with limited time and energy. As we read through the Gospels, we meet a Savior who...

- felt overwhelmed by the demands of people.

- was overcome with exhaustion from serving the constant needs upon him.

- felt the weight of the world upon his shoulders (and in a way we never will).

- wept over the effects of sin and brokenness around him, and succumbed to death himself.

Sweet sister, it's precisely because Jesus does understand that he beckons us: "Come to me, all who labor and are heavy laden, and I will give you rest" (Matthew 11:28). The Savior calls us to bring our "to do" lists, our feelings of never being enough, and the burdens we carry to him in exchange for a quiet heart. Why? Because Jesus knows what it means to be human, and he doesn't expect us to be anything other than human.

That's really good news, but what difference can it make in the real-time pressures we feel day by day?

I have often been helped by looking at some of the ways Jesus lived and responded to the expectations and pressures that he encountered during his time on earth.

JESUS UNDERSTOOD HIS PURPOSE

"For the Son of Man came to seek and to save the lost."
(Luke 19:10)

Whether Jesus was teaching, sharing a meal, or providing for people's needs, he was always seeking to love and save the lost.

In the same way, as grateful recipients of redemption, we have been called in all we do to be gospel-minded as we love and care for family members. That will look different depending on the need. For example, some days we will happily accomplish everything we hoped to do; but there will be other days when we must choose to rest in God's plan for our day even when it's far different from our own. A sick child, a hurting friend who asks to talk, or an overflowing washing machine are part of living in a fallen world, yet they also give us opportunities to rest in God's providence and grace and to love others around us with a Christ-like love.

JESUS COUNTERED LIES WITH THE TRUTH OF GOD'S WORD

When, in the wilderness, Satan sought to take advantage of Jesus' human vulnerabilities to entice him to sin, Jesus responded and resisted with the truth of God's word (Luke 4:1-13).

In our humanness, we are vulnerable to lies. Successes in our parenting might cause us to think of ourselves as self-sufficient rather than God-dependent. Difficult circumstances in life might cause us to question God's goodness and love. Comparing ourselves to others might tempt us to conclude we've failed when we have not. But God's word tells us that we need mercy (Ephesians 2:3), that we are loved (v 4-6), and that we are equipped and empowered to do all the work he has planned for us (v 8-10). When we remember that we really are only human, and we counter the lies that we can do it all by ourselves or that we cannot do it despite God's love and presence, we are free to get on with enjoying being us. It is the truth that sets us free (John 8:32).

JESUS DIDN'T ATTEMPT TO MEET EVERY NEED

Early in his ministry, crowds were looking for Jesus, but he said to his disciples, "Let us go on to the next towns, that I may preach there also, for that is why I came out" (Mark 1:38). Jesus was never too busy for people and often saw needs that others overlooked—yet he wasn't controlled by the expectations others had of him. He was able to say no.

As moms, we will always have many good opportunities and requests for help that could keep us from doing what is most important. There will always be more to do, even when it's wisest to rest. Jesus shows us the right way—that because we are human, we need to, and are free to, prioritize and even stop.

JESUS REGULARLY WENT OFF TO PRAY

After feeding more than 5,000 people and giving his disciples instructions to get into a boat, "[Jesus] went up on the mountain to pray" (Mark 6:45-46). Throughout the Gospels, we see this pattern of Jesus spending time talking to his Father.

If Jesus needed to do this, then we certainly do too! As we take everything to God in prayer, day by day, the Holy Spirit promises to guide and direct us according to his perfect will for our lives.

Sister, let this truth encourage you today: because Jesus came in human flesh, he knows exactly what it's like to feel limited and weak. Yet the Lord, who created us from dust and knows our frame, also lived a perfect life, was crucified, and rose again on our behalf. Now our Savior, who is able to sympathize with all our weaknesses, invites us to draw near to his throne of grace, that we might receive mercy and find grace to help in our times of need (Hebrews 4:14-16).

You may have superhuman expectations of others. Others may have similar expectations of you. But Jesus does not. He asks you for nothing that you cannot do. He asks you to do nothing that he does not help you with. You're only human. Jesus knows and remembers that. Be liberated from your own expectations and others' demands, and rest in the truth that, in his grace, God will not ask more of you than you have time or capacity for as you rely on him. By grace, God will equip and empower you to do all that he calls you to today.

The one who created you promises to provide all that you need to be the mother of the unique children he's blessed you with. Today you can simply rest in that.

REFLECT

- ~ As you think through ways that you are tempted to feel overwhelmed, guilty, insecure, or not enough, how does remembering that Jesus experienced the realities, limitations, and sufferings of a human body encourage you to run to him?

- ~ How does remembering that Jesus lived a perfect life of obedience on your behalf set you free from being weighed down by self-imposed burdens and the expectations of others?

Journal

EIGHT

Parenting Out of the Grace We've Received

"Folly is bound up in the heart of a child."

PROVERBS 22:15

GRACE IN A LINE

God shows me grace when I sin, so I can show the same
grace to my kids today.

A knot grew in my stomach as I hung up the phone from a call with the school. My child did what?! "There's no way," I thought. "We've taught him better than that!" But sure enough, when the truth came to light, he had done the very thing I couldn't fathom—and, worst of all, lied about it afterwards.

Every emotion from hurt, anger, and embarrassment to sadness, shock, and disappointment spun in my head. I began painting his future with the colors of this moment. By the time I had reined my thoughts back in, I'd imagined every possible scenario where this kind of behavior and choice could lead, and I'd faced a barrage of self-berating accusations over how badly I was failing as a mom.

WHAT DID I EXPECT?

Too often, this has been my gut reaction to my children's sin. Sure, I know in theory that they're sinners, but somehow, their actual sin still shocks me and sends me into a panic about where their sinful behavior could lead.

And in this particular moment, as I was mentally mapping out my child's certain future path of destruction, in the present, my son was slowly feeling crushed by the guilt, shame, and consequences of his sinful choices.

Thankfully, as I saw his anguish and heard the pain in his cries as he admitted his guilt, the Holy Spirit gently prodded me: *Sarah, remember how it felt when you saw the pain of your own sin and foolish choices—and how it still feels now. Remember the grace you've received. You've had a lifetime in which to learn and grow—why do you expect your child to be any different?*

Memories of my own choices flooded my mind—memories I often wish I could erase. But the truth is, those choices as a five-, twelve-, and 18-year-old didn't define me or dictate the rest of my future. They were a part of me growing into the woman I am today. And how I respond to my own child's sin will begin to shape how they see their sin—and the gift of the gospel.

That shift in perspective gradually softened my emotions. I had a choice. I could join Satan in heaping greater shame upon my son, as if this one act would forever define him. I could make it about myself and focus on how he hadn't lived up to my expectations, how he'd embarrassed me, and how he'd undermined my sense of being a good mom. Or I could get down on his level, as Christ would, acknowledge the sin and that consequences would have to come as a result, and remind him of the forgiveness that our gracious God always offers—forgiveness that I need just as much as my son does.

Grace didn't mean that the earthly consequences were averted. It did mean that his sin didn't have to have the last word. It did mean that when he felt the magnitude of sin's impact, it could be in light of the magnitude of God's undeserved forgiveness. What the enemy intended for evil, God was able to use for his redeeming purposes in my child's life, even through the painful consequences that came as a result.

God makes it clear in Scripture that "folly is bound up in the heart of a child" (Proverbs 22:15). We see that in our children on a daily basis, even on the best days. Our kids will sin, make unwise choices, and do things that grieve us. But as moms who are followers of Jesus, we have been given by God "a spirit not of fear but of power and love and self-control" (2 Timothy 1:7). Although we won't always respond in the most Christ-like way (and so we will need grace and forgiveness too!), we have the privilege of leading our children to the hope of the gospel and the God of all grace when they act like the sinners they are. When we expect them to be anything other than sinners, we hold them to a standard that even we can't live up to, and we forget what they most need—not to be good but to grasp God's grace and forgiveness.

FOCUS ON THE MOMENT
What I'm learning through my own parenting failures, and God's grace shown to me in return, is that our perspective of our children's sin will directly impact how we react to it

and how we shape their view of it. Instead of responding to their sin as if it will dominate the rest of their lives or define our success or failure as parents, we can ask ourselves, "How does Christ respond to my sin? Does he expect perfection out of me and then unleash his anger and disappointment when I fall short?" No, he foreknew our inability to save ourselves from our sin, and therefore he met the expectations and demands of his holiness on our behalf through his life, death, and resurrection (Romans 8:32). Now, instead of us receiving the wrath that we deserve, he treats us as beloved children. This sometimes involves us experiencing his discipline, including him allowing us to feel the painful consequences of our sin. It always means us coming to him with our shame, hurt, and guilt to receive his forgiveness and grace, and with our weakness, frailty, and fears to receive his strength and comfort.

Our sin no longer defines us. Jesus does.

We have the privilege of offering our children that same gift. If they lie, instead of saying, "I can't believe you would do such a thing!" we can explain how lying hurts our relationship because trust is broken. We can point them to Scripture, such as how Peter denied Jesus (three times!) and yet Jesus received him back and forgave him when he confessed his sin (Matthew 26:69-75; John 21:15-19). We can tell them that Jesus used that painful experience to show Peter the gospel of grace, which led him to offer gospel truth to countless others as a result—and that that same divine grace is offered to them. We can share with them how we, too, have needed Jesus' forgiveness and grace time and time again (and still do), and how God has used that to shape us to be more like Jesus.

The beauty and challenge of motherhood is that we're always learning right alongside our children. With the Spirit's help, we can be a small reflection of the grace and compassion of Christ to our children, albeit a very imperfect one. God is not a Father who looks down on us in disappointment and shame, but he "[tends to] his flock like a shepherd; he will gather the lambs in his arms; he will carry them in his bosom, and gently lead those that are with young" (Isaiah 40:11).

My fellow mom, if you're still sinning after all these years, don't expect your kids to have adult-like spiritual maturity at their young age. You still need God's grace every day. Your kids will too. So, marvel that God continues to forgive you. And that will change your heart towards your kids when they fall short too.

REFLECT

- How do you respond when your children disobey and sin?

- Next time you're faced with disappointment or concern over your child's choices, what would it look like to discipline and guide with the grace you've been shown through Christ?

Journal

NINE

The Powerful Example of Your Life

(Including When You Get it Wrong)

"Follow my example as I follow the example of Christ."

1 CORINTHIANS 11:1 (NIV)

GRACE IN A LINE

It's okay not to be perfect; my calling is to show my kids
how to rely on grace.

As I opened my Bible early one morning, attempting to spend time in God's word before my children woke up, I noticed little pen scribbles on several pages. I realized that my toddler had been imitating what she'd seen me do when I read and underlined portions of God's word while she played near me.

The apostle Paul encouraged his disciples to follow him as he followed Christ. In a similar way, God calls us to strive to be godly examples for our children to follow. It's both sobering and overwhelming to realize that little eyes are watching and hearing everything we say and do! We will likely feel our inadequacy every single day, but with God's help we can show, by our example, where we turn for wisdom in parenting and where we find grace when we fall short of being the mother we want to be.

Here are a few ways you can point your kids to Jesus day by day:

SHOW THEM WHERE TO TURN FOR WISDOM AND STRENGTH

Let your children see the importance of God's word to you. And help them learn the relevance of Scripture for their own lives. When my children were young, I did a short devotion from God's word as they ate breakfast. This would often lead to conversations about situations they faced at school, which then led to prayer. As they grew older, we used their questions and concerns as opportunities to turn to Scripture to seek God's wisdom. Car rides on the way home from church present opportunities to share the truths everyone has learned about God and how we can apply lessons in the coming week. Deuteronomy 6:4-9 directs us to use ordinary moments throughout our days to point to the Lord and his ways, making it a natural part of conversations whenever we are together. This won't look the same for everyone, and in different seasons moments like these will be more challenging to come by in a structured way—but again there's grace even in this. There's no formula to be followed, and the good news is, if you fear you've blown it while your kids were young, God can redeem years of missed opportunities.

WHEN YOU'VE BLOWN IT, MODEL THE PATH TO RESTORATION

I remember far too many days when my impatience or frustration with dawdling or disobedient children led to an irritable or angry response. Later, when I became convicted of my own sin and guilt, a spirit of discouragement and shame for another "mom-fail" would threaten to steal my joy. But the gospel says, "There is … no condemnation for those who are in Christ Jesus," (Romans 8:1). God invites us to bring our failures to the cross, assuring us that because Jesus bore our sin and shame on the cross, we can receive forgiveness and healing through the cleansing blood of our merciful Savior. "If we confess our sins, he is faithful and just to forgive us our sins and to cleanse us from all unrighteousness" (1 John 1:9). Humbled yet forgiven by God, you can then seek forgiveness from your children, using your own failures to teach them where they can turn when they sin.

WHEN THEY DISOBEY, POINT YOUR CHILDREN TO THE GOSPEL

Don't be surprised when your children sin. They are simply little sinners (Psalm 51:5) doing what sinners do. Keeping this in the forefront of your mind will help you respond more gently when your child sins in some way. While this is a time for appropriate discipline for disobedience, it is also a gospel opportunity to help them see their need for a new heart, which was purchased for them at the cross. Don't just call them to be better—point them to their Savior.

POINT YOUR CHILDREN TO GOD'S GOOD PLAN FOR MARRIAGE

The pastor John Piper reminds us of an important truth: Marriage "is designed by God to display his glory in a way that no other event or institution does … [It] is patterned after Christ's covenant relationship to his redeemed people" (*This Momentary Marriage*, Crossway, 2012, p24). Day by day, moms and dads can give their children glimpses of a biblical marriage by demonstrating how love and respect, along with grace and forgiveness, work out in relationships. Little ears hear how parents speak to one another and see how they treat each other even when they don't appear to be listening. And while children demand endless amounts of our attention, when we continue to cultivate and renew love for our spouse, we model the pattern God has established in the home.

Your marriage may not be what you hoped it would be; or it may have ended in the sadness of death or divorce. But as much as it's possible, you can show your children what it means to be faithful by looking to Christ to meet your ultimate needs and desires, as well as being appropriately faithful in whatever human relationships you have.

(As a side note, it is tragically the case that even in marriages between Christians, various forms of abuse can reside behind closed doors. Please know this is not something God calls you to endure silently in the name of "being faithful" to your spouse. While the nuances and complexities of abuse can't be addressed here, I strongly encourage you to seek godly counsel from a pastor or counselor whom you trust.)

MODEL LOVE FOR THE CHURCH

God, in his goodness, has given his people the local church, where we can gather to worship Christ and love and encourage other believers. Make sure your children see that being in and serving your church family is a priority.

MODEL THE GIFT OF PRESENCE

The older I get, the more I understand that God's greatest promise is his presence: "In your presence there is fullness of joy; at your right hand are pleasures forevermore" (Psalm 16:11). The Bible tells us that our sin hopelessly separated us from our holy God but, in love, he sent his Son to die for us to restore our relationship with him and bring us back into his presence (Romans 5:8; 1 Peter 3:18). Look for ways to help your children value the gift of presence, while pointing them to the most important friendship they can have, through a relationship with Christ.

One way we can do this is to be fully present in our homes and our children's lives. That doesn't mean we have to stay home all day; but it does mean, in a world of many distractions, being intentional about being fully present when we're together, listening to our children with good eye contact, showing interest in what's important to them, demonstrating their value as children created in the image of God. It's tempting to allow television, the phone, or the computer to become more of a presence than we are; but in a world where many people don't know how to develop genuine relationships, we give our children a great gift when we cultivate and model this in our homes.

God knows (far better than we do!) that we will fall short of being the mothers that we long to be. Yet, through the gospel of his Son, he reminds us that when we seek him in his word and prayer, run to him in repentance when we blow it, and rest in the victory he won on our behalf through Christ's death and resurrection, we can be godly examples to our children. Let your kids see you and be an example for them to follow—not of a perfect mother (she does not exist) but of an imperfect one who is growing in grace and who wants, most of all, to point her loved ones to our perfect Father.

REFLECT

- ~ What is your greatest need right now as you seek to be a godly example to your children? Whether it's a desire to read God's word or wisdom to know how to use teachable moments to point your children to the gospel, God promises to supply what we lack when we ask him.

- ~ How does God's promise to be with you encourage you in spite of your circumstances or shortcomings today?

Journal

TEN

Fighting for Your Children Through Prayer

"O our God ... we are powerless against this great horde that is coming against us. We do not know what to do but our eyes are on you."

2 CHRONICLES 20:12

GRACE IN A LINE

When I can't do anything to help my kids, God can— and I can ask him to do it.

Sarah was twelve years old and had just begun middle school when we sensed she was struggling; but we were unable to get her to share anything that could shed light on why she had started to beg to stay home from school each day. It wasn't until months had passed that it all came gushing out late one night—her 6th-grade class was populated with some socially aggressive boys who had been targeting her with sexual harassment in the guise of jesting flirtation, causing her both confusion and shame. As my husband and I held her and wiped her tears, we struggled with the emotions of anger, grief, and fear for our daughter, while feeling helpless in the face of this now-known enemy we faced.

Our budget didn't allow for Christian education, and homeschool wasn't an option as I had just taken a part-time job at our church to help defray college costs for our oldest son. We felt powerless and had no idea what to do, even while doing nothing was not an option.

We did what God's people have done through the centuries when faced with situations they felt helpless to resolve. We prayed. In the spirit of others who have been faced with overwhelming circumstances, we looked to the Old Testament king of Judah, King Jehoshaphat, who found himself facing three armies determined to destroy him and the people of Judah. 2 Chronicles tells us that he was afraid and did the only thing he knew to do in the face of pending evil: he set his face to seek the Lord and urged his people to fast and pray for God's help. The king remembered that he served the living God, who rules over all the kings of the nations. And so, he prayed:

> "O LORD, God of our fathers, are you not God in heaven? You rule over all the kingdoms of the nations. In your hand are power and might, so that none is able to withstand you … We are powerless against this great horde that is coming against us. We do not know what to do, but our eyes are on you." (20:6, 12)

King Jehoshaphat was facing a national disaster which he was powerless to avert. In our family, as Sarah's story came tumbling out, we realized that we were facing something that we had no plausible solution for. Of course our circumstances were certainly not comparable to those that faced Judah's king; but the God we spoke to was exactly the same as the God to whom Jehoshaphat made his plea—the same living God, in whose hand is all power and might. We ran to him with all our fears, anger, and uncertainties about how to protect this vulnerable daughter of ours in a way that honored God. And we asked others to pray that God would give us wisdom, faith, and patience to trust him and walk in his power by faith.

As we turned to God in prayer, we sensed that this was the question that confronted us:

> *Did we trust both God's power to help and his goodness and love for us in bringing us into these circumstances?*

Our answer mattered because, unless our confidence was in the Lord alone, we would either turn to what seemed wise in our own eyes and seek worldly solutions rather than trusting God's wisdom, or we would fall into a kind of hopeless despair. So we reminded ourselves from God's word that we could pray with confidence to the one who rules over all things. To Jehoshaphat, God said, "Do not be afraid, and do not be dismayed at this great horde, for the battle is not yours but God's. Stand firm, hold your position, and see the salvation of the Lord on your behalf" (v 15). We realized that we, too, were being called to stand firm in our faith and to trust in God's help as we looked to him.

We took heart, too, from the time when Jesus' disciples felt powerless as their boat was swamped by waves during a great storm on a lake. They cried out to Jesus (who was asleep in the boat):

> *"'Save us, Lord; we are perishing.' And he said to them, 'Why are you afraid, O you of little faith?' Then he rose*

and rebuked the winds and the sea, and there was a great calm." (Matthew 8:23-27)

As we faced this "storm" in our family, God was again calling us to trust him.

And in God's time and way, he faithfully brought us through that battle against our daughter's soul.

It would not be the last time we would face what felt like "a great horde" coming against us, but it served to cultivate a deeper sense of our need to run straight into the arms of our heavenly Father at all times. It is easy to forget this when we are busy or tired or feel like we can handle things on our own. And so it is a gift of God to be confronted with our own helplessness—these times are blessings if they bring us to our knees before the God who is all-powerful and works all things "together for good, for those who are called according to his purpose" (Romans 8:28).

As a mom, you will always have more than enough to do, and you will therefore always have a reason not to pray. But you will never have sufficient reason not to, for every day, on good days and bad, what your children need more is not your protection and guidance but the Lord's. Resolve to be a mom who prays—a mom who enjoys the gift of lifting things to our Father, who is powerful and kind:

~ Pray because God commands it as the way to communicate your love, trust, and need for his help. (Philippians 4:4-7)

~ Pray because God draws near to those who humbly look to him. (Isaiah 66:2; 1 Peter 5:6-7)

~ Pray because the Lord loves you and your children,

and knows better than you do what we need to be saved and find everlasting joy in Christ. (Matthew 6:33; Proverbs 3:5-6)

~ Pray because it reminds you that as a finite creature, you are dependent on God for everything. (Isaiah 41:13; Proverbs 16:9; Psalm 121:1-2)

~ Pray because it's only by God's grace, through his Spirit, that you are kept safe from walking in the wisdom of the world, which always leads to death rather than life. (Psalm 91; Matthew 6:13; Psalm 9:9-10)

Pray like this and you can be confident that God will answer—not necessarily in the way you wish or in the timing you would choose but in the way that, if you could see what he can see, you would know is for the best.

In other words, pray as Jehoshaphat did:

~ trusting God

~ humbly acknowledging your inability and need

~ knowing that God loves his people and is committed to their salvation and everlasting joy

~ recognizing your dependence on God's powerful intervention

~ accepting that it is only by God's grace that his people are saved

Parenting crises will inevitably come. In those moments when you don't know what to do, keep your eyes on God. He loves to help those who call upon him, and he is able to do far more than you can ask or imagine (Ephesians 3:20-21)! He can change what you cannot and heal what you cannot. And when the crises are past and life feels easier again, don't forget the lessons learned. God gives wisdom, counsel, and strength to those who run to him in prayer. The best thing you can do for your children is to be a praying, dependent, trusting mom, on the best of days as well as the worst.

REFLECT

- ~ What did you learn about God from Jehoshaphat's prayer? How does this motivate you to pray for your children?

- ~ Where do you currently see your need for God's wisdom and help in the midst of perplexing or overwhelming circumstances?

Journal

ELEVEN

When My Child Hurts

"It was not that this man sinned, or his parents, but that the works of God might be displayed in him."

JOHN 9:3

GRACE IN A LINE

God can use my children's struggles to bring them closer to him, which is the best thing that can happen to them.

The only thing worse than your own pain is watching your child suffer. We often feel so helpless to do anything about it, and we bear the role of trying to help our child wrestle with the challenges and questions that suffering provokes—questions that we're often still trying to grapple with ourselves.

I will never forget my daughter, curled up on the couch as pain plagued her little body, looking up at me with a tear-streaked face and saying, "Mom, I don't want to hurt your feelings, but if you were sick before you had kids, why did you have children if it would make us sick too? And if you didn't know, then why did God allow it?"

I didn't know when I was having children that I had a

disease that could be passed on to them. And I knew my sweet daughter wasn't trying to hurt me. She was genuinely wrestling with difficult and complex questions.

But how was I supposed to answer her? It felt so unfair. Why couldn't she just enjoy the innocence of being a child instead of having to worry about swallowing pills, countless appointments, and squirming in her chair at school as she tried to hide her aching joints? I shared her question. And, even more than that, I wanted an answer, and I desperately wanted to free her from the pain that provoked her questions in the first place.

Can you relate? If so, I'm incredibly sorry. We all want to protect our kids from suffering, and we hurt deeply with them when trials come. I can't take that pain away. But I hope to encourage you with the ways the Lord has encouraged and strengthened me when my children have been hurting.

OUR VIEW OF SUFFERING WILL SHAPE OUR CHILDREN'S

In John 9, the disciples and Jesus were walking past a man who had been born blind. The disciples asked Jesus directly, "Rabbi, who sinned, this man or his parents, that he was born blind" (John 9:2)? Much like we often do, they wanted to understand the cause. If we know the cause, then maybe we can do something to stop it or avoid it. At the very least, the nagging "Why?" question will disappear. And in this case, the disciple's immediate assumption was that someone had to be at fault—either the blind man or his parents.

But here's what I love—Jesus turns their whole perspective of suffering on its head in his response:

> *"It was not that this man sinned, or his parents, but that the works of God might be displayed in him."*

While the disciples were racking their brains to find an earthly answer, God was reminding them that his purposes are often far higher than our finite minds can comprehend. While we want to know the cause of our children's suffering so that we can spare them from it or at least answer their questions about it, God wants us to see our children's suffering through the lens of his character and truth so that he can work in it to display his character and glory to and through our kids.

What trials are your children facing right now? Whatever they may be, I can guarantee you this—God isn't allowing it because he's heartless or he lacks the ability to prevent it. Although he may not give you an earthly reason why, he does assure you that it isn't pointless or accidental. He may very well be allowing this pain because his long-view love for your child knows that not saving them from temporary heartache is the path to saving their soul for eternity with him. He will only allow what he must to draw them into his saving grace, so that his works might be displayed (Lamentations 3:33).

The question is: do we view the pain of our children with the same perspective?

Naturally, we don't. (Or at least, I don't.) Naturally, I respond to my children's pain in the same way as I do my own. I want ease, comfort, success. I want answers. I want heaven on earth.

But what if I knew that blissful happiness and health for the next seven decades would be the very things that would prevent my children from knowing Christ and the eternal healing he brings? Would I then still desire most a pain-free life for them?

I don't ask this lightly because I know the deep pain of watching a child suffer. But deep down, as Christian parents we do know that our kids' eternal salvation is far more important than their temporary comfort. And yet, if we're honest with ourselves, do we live like we believe that, or do we live as though every disappointment, hurt feeling, and health issue is the greatest threat to our children?

Do we believe God knows what's best for our children, even when it doesn't seem best from our limited perspective? Do we believe he can redeem what seems hopeless? Do we believe he is good and faithful? Do we trust that Jesus can provide what our child needs, even when we don't know what those needs are? Do we believe God can use their suffering to draw them to him, grow their character, and glorify himself through their lives?

These are crucial questions because how we answer them will drastically change what we value for our children, including the priorities we set, the decisions we make, and the responses we have to the painful circumstances that come into their lives.

If you aren't sure you can truthfully answer these questions with "yes" right now, be honest with God about that. After all, he already knows the fears that grip your heart. But know this: just as God wants to work in your child through their sufferings, he is at work in you through their pain as well. You can come to Christ in honesty and ask him to grow in you a deeper heart of faith as you seek to help your child do the same.

HIDDEN TREASURE IN UNWANTED PLACES

It will always be difficult to see our children endure difficulty. But, in God's grace, he can redeem it by making them into vessels that display his goodness, faithfulness, and power.

We will still ache at the sight of their tears—but those tears may open their eyes to the truth that this world is not their home and that Jesus came not only to die for their sins but to carry their sorrows.

We won't have all the answers to their questions—but their trials will teach them to wrestle with deep spiritual truths that many adults have yet to grapple with.

We won't be able to control the outcomes—but we can learn to be less gripped by fear of what we can't control, and to trust that their lives are in the hands of a good and faithful God.

We can still pray for their relief, healing, and protection—but we can also pray that God will not waste the pain in their lives and will only allow what he will use for their ultimate good.

And in our humanity, when our children hurt, we may still give way to fear, grasp for control, plead for changed circumstances, and battle discouragement. But God's grace meets us there too.

So if you find yourself navigating a difficult road with your child, you are not alone. From one mom to another, I want to say this to you: this is far from easy. You are likely having to learn these difficult truths right alongside your child. But you can bring your fears, worries, and anguish to Jesus, who sees, knows, and loves you and your children intimately. You may not be able to control the challenges that come into their lives or feel equipped to handle them, but you can trust the one who draws near and says, "Fear not, for I am with you; be not dismayed, for I am your God; I will strengthen you, I will help you, I will uphold you with my righteous right hand" (Isaiah 41:10).

And you can pray a brave, faith-filled prayer: that God will use every single difficulty that comes into your children's lives to awaken their spiritual senses of compassion, empathy, humility, self-control, perseverance, and gratitude, and, above all, their need for a Savior. What greater joy could there be than for us to see our children come to know Christ and display the works of God through their lives—whatever the cost.

REFLECT

- Do you fear pain and difficulty coming into your child's life? What are you most afraid of?

- Do you believe God is sovereign over everything he allows in your children's lives? Can you see how a difficult circumstance in your child's life (or yours) has proven to shape and grow them (or you) in positive ways?

Journal

TWELVE

The Facade of Super-Mom

"Come to me, all who labor and are heavy laden, and I will give you rest. Take my yoke upon you, and learn from me, for I am gentle and lowly in heart, and you will find rest for your souls. For my yoke is easy, and my burden is light."

MATTHEW 11:28-30

GRACE IN A LINE

Jesus doesn't ask me or need me to be super-mom.
I'm free to say no when I need to.

I stared at the little box next to the words "Check here to join the school PTA." As I filled out my child's school registration, I felt the tension rise within me. Good moms get involved at their child's school, I thought. I'm already overwhelmed with what's on my plate, but everyone I know is volunteering. What does it say about me if I don't?

Those little boxes are around every corner. Sign here to coach your child's team. Check here to help arrange school activities. Sign here to be on the church welcoming committee. Check here to join our gym membership. Click here to learn how to cook healthy meals for your family. Check here to register for homeschooling materials. Sign here to join the company that allows you to work from home and still make money!

It's exhausting, isn't it? I feel stressed just thinking about it. So many of us ceaselessly strive to keep up with endless demands and give everything our best.

Of course, it's good to check "yes" in any of these boxes. It's wonderful and helpful to be involved in our children's education; it's good to be invested in our church by volunteering; it's good and right to do what we can to take care of the bodies God has given us; it can be a wonderful option for some moms to homeschool their children; equally, there are many moms who either feel called to work or have to do so out of necessity.

The problem arises when we come to believe that we should be able to do it all, be it all, and look good doing it. We look at others who seem like they're doing just that—but we can't necessarily see that there's always a cost somewhere. No one truly can do it all. Supermom may appear to be everything you can't live up to, but she may also be exhausted, unhappy, or "doing it all" at the expense of her marriage, health, or spiritual rest.

Sister, if I could pull up a chair beside you, I'd give you a cup of tea (or coffee) and encourage your weary heart by saying, "Lay down your striving to do and be it all, and quiet the lies that tell you that you're less of a mom because you can't. Take a deep breath and give yourself a heavy dose of grace—because God does."

Rest in this truth: every mom has unique capacities and circumstances.

When I stared at the dreaded box to join the school PTA, I had a choice. I could look at the woman next to me checking "yes" and decide to overstretch myself in an unhealthy way. I could check "no" but then beat myself up as I told myself I was falling short of the mom I should be.

Or, I could remember that the mom next to me may not be navigating an extremely difficult special-needs child, chronic health issues, or a husband who was working away from home most of the time. I could remember that she may simply have more energy and need less sleep than me. I could remember that I am not saved by saying yes to everything, and I am free to say no when that is wisest for me, in my specific circumstances.

ALL IN BALANCE

This is not a freedom to say no to everything, though! Galatians 6:2 calls us to "bear one another's burdens," referring to the weighty trials and troubles that come upon us—but verse 5 then clarifies that we're also called to "each ... bear his own load," which refers to the basic God-given responsibilities we've each been given. How that may look practically will vary for each of us to some extent, but as moms, we each have a load that we're called to bear—to faithfully love and serve our families with the strength God equips us with. Coming to Jesus to receive his rest doesn't equate to kicking back, putting up our feet, and saying no to anything that stretches or challenges us.

For example, there are many days when my body is begging me to sit down and not move another muscle. Sometimes, it's wise for me to humble myself and ask for help. But often, I need to ask the Lord to give me the strength one step at a time to carry my load as a mom in the typical daily duties of raising a family, partnering with my husband in teaching and training our kids in the truth of Scripture, transporting them to and from activities, and following through on commitments. I'm often ready to collapse by the time bedtime comes around, but it's important to temporarily set aside my desire for rest in order to tuck my kids into bed, pray with them, and be a listening ear to their questions (which always seem to come the moment I'm trying to close their bedroom door for the night!). Although there will be extenuating circumstances at times, they should be the exception to the norm, rather than the norm, as we seek to honor the Lord with the responsibilities that are ours to bear (with God's help).

FINDING REST IN CHRIST

What, then, does Jesus mean by "Come to me, all who labor and are heavy-laden, and I will give you rest"?

It means we are invited to clothe ourselves daily in the truth of the gospel—we are invited to remember that our standing before God is not dependent on how many good things we're doing or how well we're doing them. We are forgiven, accepted, and loved because Christ lived the perfect life we cannot and paid for our sins, failures, and weaknesses on our behalf. If you are a child of God, you are received and loved by your heavenly Father because Jesus has called you his own, not because you are doing as much as the mom next door. This is what enables you to work hard as a mom, to make sacrifices for your family, and to persevere through the countless ups and downs of motherhood, yet at the same time to be freed from the lie that good moms always say yes. God does not ask you to be a supermom, and so you do not need to demand it of yourself.

Sister, rest in that today. Cease striving to be something you can't be and aren't called to be. And ask the Holy Spirit to grant you the wisdom and discernment to rest in Jesus and to be faithful where he has you right now—even if that looks like checking "no" in the PTA box.

REFLECT

- When you examine your life right now, are there areas in which you have stretched yourself thin in an attempt to "do it all"? Are you feeling weary over all that's on your plate or battling guilt over what you aren't doing? If so, pray and ask God to give you wisdom as to where he wants you right now and where you can be free to step back or say no in this season.

Journal

_____
_____
_____
_____
_____
_____
_____
_____
_____
_____
_____
_____
_____
_____
_____
_____
_____
_____
_____
_____
_____

THIRTEEN

What Motherhood Teaches Us about God

"See what kind of love the Father has given to us, that we should be called children of God."

1 JOHN 3:1

GRACE IN A LINE

God loves me even more than I love my kids.

I remember the moment my son was placed into my arms for the first time. As I gazed into his tiny face, an overwhelming sense of love for this miracle coursed through me, and I knew my life would never be the same. Before we had even left the hospital, God had given me a glimpse of his unconditional love for his beloved children:

> *"'For the mountains may depart and the hills be removed, but my steadfast love shall not depart from you, and my covenant of peace shall not be removed,' says the* LORD, *who has compassion on you." (Isaiah 54:10)*

But while my firstborn was compliant, slept well, and smiled at anyone who came near, my second child was far more challenging. Colic kept him (and me!) from sleeping much for the first few months; he would scream for hours on end, and he wouldn't let anyone hold him but me. Through this child, God had different things he wanted me to learn about his love. It was as I navigated my way through days of laughter and tears, joys and sorrows, exhilaration and defeats that God faithfully taught me about his steadfast love for me.

1 John 3:1 invites us to see what kind of love God has for us, that we should be called his children. His love for us is merciful, unconditional, compassionate, forgiving, and patient—a love that is seen most clearly of all through him sending Jesus Christ to save sinners. His love for us is a perfect, parental love. And through each season of parenting, God grants mothers opportunities to be both recipients of and reflections of his love for his children:

GOD'S LOVE PURSUES REBELS

"But God shows his love for us in that while we were still sinners, Christ died for us." (Romans 5:8)

One day my teenaged daughter looked me in the eye and said, "Why can't you be more like my friends' moms? I never want to be like you!" By God's grace, I grabbed her in a fierce hug and said, "No matter how much you push me away, Sarah, I will never stop loving you and fighting for you!" To my surprise, she collapsed in my arms and began sobbing. The battles would rage on for a while, but because I was able to respond with the love of Christ (that time—I did not always get it right), my daughter knew in that moment that my love was stronger than her rebellion.

The same is true for us with God. Ephesians 2:1-3 essentially pictures us taking a similar stance to the one my daughter took against me. By nature, we want God on our own terms, not his. We are rebellious and don't want him. "But God, being rich in mercy, because of the great love with which he loved us" saved us from ourselves (v 4). Why? So that we might be seated in his presence and enjoy his riches and his kindness for eternity (v 6-7).

God's love was stronger than your rebellion—so he brought you to faith. God's love is stronger than your struggles—so he works in you by his Spirit. God's love is stronger than any hurdle—so he will bring us safely home to himself one day. Our very best moments of motherly love are just a glimpse of the kind and quality of love he pours out for us.

GOD'S LOVE PROTECTS

"Because he holds fast to me in love, I will deliver him; I will protect him, because he knows my name."
(Psalm 91:14)

My natural motherly instinct is to protect my children. My Father's love is likewise a protective love. The Lord is our shepherd—he doesn't always shield us from danger (although often he does!), but he guides us down the path that will lead to ultimate and eternal joy in his presence. As a mom, I've needed to protect my children from known dangers that they can't see. I've needed them to know that they can always run to me. The more I've learned of God's love, the more I can confidently say, "[The Lord is] my refuge and my fortress, my God, in whom I trust" (v 2).

GOD'S LOVE DISCIPLINES

"For the Lord disciplines the one he loves, and chastises every son whom he receives." (Hebrews 12:6)

It doesn't take long as mothers before we realize that the seemingly innocent child we gave birth to is in reality a sinner, by nature and by choice. It also doesn't take long to see what happens to a child left to their own unrestrained selfish desires. Parents who love their children set boundaries for their children; and parents who love will use appropriate and loving discipline when those boundaries are crossed.

In a world that often confuses discipline with punishment, it's important to remember that God's discipline is always an extension of his fatherly love. The one God disciplines and teaches is blessed (Psalm 94:12)! Sometimes he uses natural consequences to help us course-correct; other times he uses afflictions as a tool to accomplish his good purposes in our lives. But even when his discipline feels severe, we can be confident that the God who suffered and died on the cross for us always has our eternal joy in view.

As a mother, the more I understand that God disciplines and allows affliction out of love, the faster I am able, by his grace, to submit to his discipline when it comes in my own life. At the same time, as we grow in understanding God's loving purposes in discipline, that will shape the reasons and ways that we discipline our own beloved children—fairly, consistently, never harshly, always humbly.

GOD DELIGHTS IN RELATIONSHIP

"The LORD your God is in your midst, a mighty one who will save; he will rejoice over you with gladness; he will

quiet you by his love; he will exult over you with loud singing." (Zephaniah 3:17)

Just as we (when we're at our best) enjoy spending time with our children and delight in seeing ourselves in them, so our Father in heaven delights in his relationship with us, glimpsing his image in us! It can seem hard to believe, but the truth is that our Creator has redeemed us for the very purpose of enjoying a relationship with us forever. He is already delighting in us now! God helps us experience some of his delight in us by giving us joy in our own children. When you sing to a child in the night, quiet a fretful child on your lap, or comfort a child when they've been hurt, you are catching a glimmer of God's love for you, while also pointing your children to his love for them.

GOD DELIGHTS IN OUR EXPRESSIONS OF TRUST

"O LORD of hosts, blessed is the one who trusts in you!"
(Psalm 84:12)

"For this is the love of God, that we keep his commandments." (1 John 5:3)

There are countless times in parenting when we must ask our children to trust in our love and wisdom because we know that giving them what they want would not benefit them in the long run. And we want our children's obedience to the boundaries we set to be based on their trust of us because they know that we want what is best for them, even when it's different than what they would have chosen for themselves.

In the same way, God asks us to trust in his love when he says no or not yet, even when that makes no sense to us. We demonstrate our trust by obeying his word even when it's hard, assured that he will always ask from us and do for us what will best serve our eternal joy. In those moments when we realize our children trust us we are being pointed to how we can enjoy the love of our own Father—by trusting in his heart as he leads us through life.

Whenever you express love to your children today, use those moments as reminders of God's love for you. Let your love for them be guided by his love for you, and let your love for them deepen your appreciation of his perfect love for you. For however great the love that you have for your children may be, it cannot compare to the incomprehensible love God has for his children—for you.

REFLECT

- In what ways have you come to see and appreciate God's love through your own love for your children?

- How does God's desire for relationship encourage you to draw near to him?

Journal

FOURTEEN

Souls, Sufferers, and Sinners

"You search out my path and my lying down and are acquainted with all my ways."

PSALM 139:3

GRACE IN A LINE

God knows and treats me and my kids as the real, complex people we are.

Underneath every emotion, decision, and action there are countless factors at play. My reaction to the loud laughter and squeals of my children can evoke a smile on my face as I watch them burst with the simple pleasures of childhood. But on a day when I'm not feeling well or I'm overwhelmed by the mess around me or the argument I had with my husband, my reaction to that same circumstance may be one of agitation and annoyance. My body hears the same noise, but my mind and soul respond differently.

And, just like me and you, our children are complex beings too.

ALL THREE AT ONCE

Aside from God's word, I've found the most helpful framework for seeing my children and those around me is Mike Emlet's explanation of how each Christian is a saint (or "soul" can be used if we are thinking of those who are not Christians), a sufferer, and a sinner. All three realities are intertwined with one another, which we see throughout Scripture:

- *Saints:* "To those sanctified in Christ Jesus, called to be saints together with all those who in every place call upon the name of our Lord Jesus Christ, both their Lord and ours." (1 Corinthians 1:2)

- *Sufferers:* "And after you have suffered a little while, the God of all grace, who has called you to his eternal glory in Christ, will himself restore, confirm, strengthen, and establish you." (1 Peter 5:10)

- *Sinners:* "For all have sinned and fall short of the glory of God." (Romans 3:23)

I've found this to be helpful in three ways...

1. HOW WE VIEW OURSELVES

At any given moment, there are numerous factors affecting how we think, feel, and respond. One of those is suffering. If we've had a difficult day, we're grieving the loss of a loved one, or we're sick, it will impact every part of us. And that suffering can leave us more vulnerable to temptation. Yes, we're still accountable for our sin, but we're also finite beings with weaknesses and limitations, living in a fallen world. Without excusing our sinful reaction, it's wise to recognize that we may need to sleep or rest, to process something that we're going through with a sister in Christ or get some physical exercise. Even Jesus recognized his human limitations, saying no at times in order to spend time with his Father or get the rest his body and mind needed (Mark 6:31).

Nevertheless, it remains the case that tangled within our weaknesses and suffering are sinful desires and responses—sin that we can't excuse or ignore simply because we're tired or hurting. Even when we're more vulnerable to temptation (just as Jesus was in the wilderness), we still need to call sin what it is and repent of it to the Lord and anyone else we've sinned against. We are not only sufferers—we're also sinners.

But, more than anything, if we are trusting in Jesus, we're saints. The Lord doesn't see you primarily as the woman who snapped at her children or the woman who is suffering from weariness so much that she can't finish her to-do list. No, he looks at you as his beloved daughter, who he is singing over (Zephaniah 3:17). He is not tolerating you; he is delighting in you. That's grace.

2. HOW WE VIEW OUR CHILDREN

Each child is uniquely wired. Some are pragmatic; others are more emotional. Some struggle to express themselves; others wear their emotions on their sleeve. Each is influenced by varying factors in their little world—circumstances, the actions or moods of those around them, their physical needs, sinful desires, or how they perceive the world around them.

For example, when one of my sons was younger and his brain struggled to regulate, one small stressor (such as being overstimulated in a crowd) could send him spiraling. He would suddenly erupt, far beyond anyone's ability to talk to him rationally. But he wasn't just an angry kid who needed to get his act together. He was a soul who was suffering because of his illness, and he was at war with sin, all at the same time. Being stern with him in frustration wouldn't help him regulate his emotions, and only addressing his sinful response wouldn't serve either of us well. Seeing him as a whole person meant that I needed first to help him regulate his mind and body, which were beyond his control in that moment. Once he was calm, then I could gently point out the sin that had surfaced, remind him of tools he could use to help himself avoid losing control next time, and remind him that he could turn to Jesus for forgiveness and help, because that is what saints do.

Thankfully, God doesn't leave us to our own resources, and he promises to give wisdom when we ask. When you feel your limitations in knowing and understanding your child's heart and all the complexities surrounding it, the greatest gift you can give them is the hope of Jesus—because he is the only one who fully understands them and is able to bring the comfort, healing, and forgiveness they need (Isaiah 53:5).

3. HOW WE SHAPE OUR CHILDREN'S VIEW OF OTHERS

Although we want to raise our children to be discerning, we're not to judge "by appearances, but judge with right judgment" (John 7:24). However, because our natural bent is to make rash judgments, we need to teach our children to judge rightly with the lens of the grace—a lens that sees others as more than their actions or appearances. They, too, are people—souls, sufferers, and sinners.

For example, a classmate who's bullying other children, a teen who's turned to drugs, or a kid at church who's bragging about sleeping around is a sinner. Just like everyone else, unless they put their faith in Christ, they will be held accountable to God because they are sinners by nature and choice. We are no better than them. It's crucial that we emphasize to our kids that, although their classmate is going against God's good will and loving commands, each one of us, apart from God's common grace, is capable of any sin. And in the end, all unrepented sin will be judged rightly and fully.

At the same time, we can remind our kids that their classmate is also a sufferer living in a fallen world, with a body and mind that's been impacted by the fall. They may have countless reasons why they act in the way they do (unhealthy home life, trauma, insecurity, mental-health challenges, and so on), and we'd likely have greater compassion if we knew what was going on under the surface of their actions.

But most importantly, they are a soul—an image-bearer of God who has been blinded by the enemy and the sin of this world. Like all of us before the grace of God opened our eyes to the truth, they're seeking a place in which to belong, something to fill the void in their life, and a purpose to live for. They need a Savior and a hope just as much as we do. And we have the privilege of being an example of Christ's compassion, grace, and love to them, even as we hold firm to the truth of Scripture.

None of this means that we excuse the sin of others. But, if we shift the narrative to help our children see beyond the surface of other's choices, it will help grow in them a compassion that sees each person as someone made in the image of God—a soul who longs to be known and loved, a sufferer trying to endure this world apart from the hope of Christ, and a sinner who needs a Savior.

Sisters, we're all in this camp—we are saints, sufferers, and sinners living with and among saints (souls), sufferers, and sinners. God has compassion on our frailty as these three realities play a role in our journey of motherhood. And this lens can help you to see each of your children as a sinner who needs a Savior, a sufferer who needs our compassion and patience, and a soul who needs the hope and healing of Christ—and treat them not just as one of those categories but all three.

What a beautiful picture of God's grace to us, our children, and those around us.

REFLECT

- Think of a circumstance in your life right now. How do these three realities (saint, sufferer, sinner) play a role in impacting you emotionally, physically, and spiritually?

- Now think of a situation with your child. Can you see how these three realities have impacted their reaction, emotions, and perspective? What might it look like to address them as a whole and complex being, rather than simply respond to what you see on the surface?

Journal

FIFTEEN

For Such a Time as This

"And who knows whether you have not come to the
kingdom for such a time as this."

ESTHER 4:14

GRACE IN A LINE

God has deliberately put my kids in this time and place,
and he has a purpose for them.

I don't have to tell you how much there is to fear as parents raising children in a complex world. While there are countless things that are great about growing up in the 2020s, there are also many things we wouldn't choose for our kids to be facing: the pervasiveness of pornography, social-media bullying, gender confusion, rising suicide rates, drugs, child predators, indoctrination from all angles… I could go on. I don't know about you, but I find myself feeling fearful over all I need to protect my children from and equip them for.

So it's easy to wish our kids could have been raised in some other decade that looks (from our limited perspective), well, easier. But whichever decade you'd choose to raise your kids in if you could, you would certainly never choose one from the 5th century BC, in which the Old Testament story of Esther is set.

NOT THE EASIEST OF TIMES

Taken from her home and orphaned at some point, Esther was forced to live in Babylon—in the capital city of the enemies of God's people. She was then objectified, picked out to sleep with the king for her beauty, and then made to marry him—the same king who had just banished his previous wife simply because she'd done something he thought was disrespectful while he was drunk. Then things became harder— she was faced with the threat of the massacre of her people and told that she alone had a chance to put a stop it, even though the attempt might cost her her life.

Like I said, not the time or the place in which you'd choose to raise your children.

But her cousin, Mordecai, who had raised her and was her father figure, hadn't had a choice. And when he heard of the plan to slaughter all God's people throughout the Babylonian Empire, he begged Esther to use her position to plead for the king's intervention to save her people. They both knew that to do that would carry the very grave threat of death since no one was allowed to enter the king's gates without being summoned by him.

Yet, Mordecai pointed out, "Who knows whether you have not come to the kingdom *for such a time as this*" (Esther 4:14, emphasis added).

Mordecai knew that none of these events were out of God's control. And he sensed that God had brought Esther to that place, at that exact time, for the saving of many.

As the story unfolds, Esther courageously and wisely plans how to approach the king, and God sovereignly moves the heart of the king to show her favor, saving her and her people as a result. God had indeed ordained the days of Esther's life "for such a time as this," to accomplish his saving purposes through her.

Friend, God has also placed you and me, and the children whom he's entrusted to us, on this earth "for such a time as this." The way our world is right now is not a surprise to him. So, instead of living in fear about the world our children are growing up in, we can find comfort in knowing that God has given them life and breath at this time in history for a reason.

The truth is that there has never been an easy time to follow Christ in a world that hates him and all those who follow him. The most important thing for our kids is that they grow to commit their lives to Jesus no matter what the cost and put God's glory before their comfort. God has good plans for his children—and let's pray that his children includes our kids—in the time and place in which he's put them. That may include them taking risks, courting danger, and experiencing hardship. We don't see the end of the story yet (and neither, in the midst of the crisis, did Esther).

So what our kids need from us is that we raise them not in a way that simply protects them from the realities of living in a fallen world, but in a way that equips them to live radically and purposefully in a world that desperately needs the hope of Jesus.

EQUIPPING OUR CHILDREN

The story of Esther also offers some truths that we can apply to ourselves as moms as we raise our children in this very different but still difficult time in history. Here are a few practical applications that have helped shape my own parenting.

1. LET YOUR CHILDREN DO HARD THINGS

If we want resilient, persevering, God-fearing children who are willing to live boldly for the truth (like Esther), we have to be willing to give room for the Spirit to do his sanctifying work in their lives, even if they must face temporary discomfort for that to happen. We can and should be a comfort, guide, and support along the way, but let's make sure we are in a way that teaches our children to make wise choices, learn from failure, and run to Christ as their ultimate hope. Don't shield them from everything that is hard—support them in dealing with what is hard.

2. RAISE CRITICAL THINKERS

As Christian parents, we can be driven by fear to frantically shove as much knowledge and as many "answers" down our children's throats as we possibly can, just hoping they will stick and keep them on the straight and narrow.

But if we don't teach our children to think critically for themselves, what will they do when we're no longer there to tell them how to think and act? If we simply enforce obedience to authority without helping them understand why and what they're obeying, then how will they be equipped to understand that there are times when it's right to disobey an authority that's leading them to disobey God, their ultimate authority? If Esther had avoided entering the king's chamber out of fear for her own safety or obedience to her earthly ruler, she would have missed out on the privilege of being the vessel God used to save his people. But she did go in, because Esther had the wisdom and boldness to disobey her earthly king for the sake of obeying her heavenly one.

If we take the time to help our children understand why and how God's word shapes what we do and say, and encourage them to think for themselves about how it applies to their particular time and place, then they will learn to think for themselves and measure their thoughts and opinions against God's word, rather than simply what they're being told to believe. Our children need to learn to think and discern, not just to react.

3. PRAY FERVENTLY FOR THEIR HEARTS

We can't possibly know all that threatens our children or the inner workings of each of their hearts. But just as Mordecai fasted and prayed on behalf of Esther as she approached the king (Esther 4:15-17), we have the incredible privilege of bringing our fears, requests, and need for wisdom to our heavenly Father on behalf of our children. We don't have the power to bring a dead heart to life, protect our children from serious harm, or determine their future—but we have direct access to the one who does.

Sister, the story of Esther and the witness of Scripture teach us to say no to fearing for our children's future as though God is not in control and will not prevail. But they also teach us to say no to a complacent assumption that they'll be fine, as though God does not call us to equip them to take risks, think wisely, and pray dependently (and, above all, to teach them the gospel). As you consider the culture today and its direction in the future, you can know that God is sovereign and that he has a purpose for your kids in the time and place he's chosen to put them in. With the help of the Spirit, you can work (in dependence rather than panic) towards showing your kids why and how they can live and love like Christ in "such a time as this."

REFLECT

- What fears grip you as a mom? Do you see ways in which you're tempted to parent or overprotect in response to that fear, rather than trust?

- What encouragement do you find in the truth that your child has been ordained to live in this time and place in history—and in your specific family? How might that reality change the way you parent?

Journal

SIXTEEN

A Mother's Prayer

GRACE IN A LINE

There's nothing that my Father doesn't want me to talk to him about.

*L*ord, thank you for the gift of being a mom. I know there are days when I don't fully appreciate the amazing privilege it is to raise the children you've entrusted to me, but I know that each one is a gift from you—a gift that many long for but not all receive.

I praise you for how unique you've made each child from head to toe, all with distinctive personalities, strengths, and stories being written daily in front of me. In your power and wisdom, you knit each one together in my womb, breathing life into their lungs and purpose into their beating heart. Give me eyes to see the miracle that they are.

Thank you for the precious moments that I get to experience as a mom. From the moment they were placed in my arms to their beaming faces as they took their first steps; from the sweet sound of giggles and "I love yous" to the day they took their first steps of mature independence. May I always have the eyes to see the gift that these moments are, and never forget them.

Father, I admit that I too often take my children for granted. I know that too often I treat them as an inconvenience or interruption. Forgive me for my moments of impatience, for being short-tempered, for being distracted, for using rash words, for harshness in discipline at times, and at other times for a lack of needed discipline. So often, I fall short of being the mom I want to be. And yet, all this reminds me that I need your help, strength, and wisdom every single day.

Lord, as thankful as I am to be a mom, I can also be paralyzed by fear, guilt, and the belief that their earthly and eternal future is solely up to me. It's easy either to distract myself with meaningless things to avoid the weight of responsibility or to meticulously try to control everything around them out of fear. Oh Lord, help me love and lead them well!

May your grace cover all that I cannot know or control.

Please guard my children's hearts from my sin, weaknesses, and failings. Please do not allow these flaws in me to lead them away from you. Instead, draw them to you and, by your grace, save them from a life of wandering and rebellion and loving the world more than you. Whatever it takes, draw their hearts to you, save them from their sin, and bring them into your kingdom! Although you alone can change their hearts, help me to teach, train, and love them in a way that points them to your saving grace each and every day.

Father, protect their hearts and minds in a world that's filled with evil, violence, and countless things to fear. As much as I wish I could protect them from any and all pain—physical, mental, and spiritual—I know that I am limited in my ability and wisdom to do so. But I trust that you know what's best for these precious children. I thank you that you love them more and better than I ever could. Please protect them from anything that will not lead them to you and only allow what will be used for their good and your glory. Help me to trust you when you allow pain and circumstances that I can't make sense of.

May your grace cover my children's hearts and lives.

I confess my tendency to compare my children, family, and motherhood to those of women around me. Every time I scroll through social media, I see countless family resources and activities and wonder if I'm doing enough. I see the accolades and successes of other children and feel the sting of comparison. I see pictures of beautiful decor and organized houses and wonder why I am the only one struggling to keep my children fed and clothed, let alone keeping an immaculate house. I see families who are all smiles on vacation and wonder if my children are being deprived of a good life when we have less to give them. When I walk through church and see well-behaved children walking in matching outfits like little ducklings behind their mom, I'm embarrassed by the fact that one of my children came to church without shoes and we're all still recovering from the dispute that erupted in the back of the car on the ride over.

May your grace wash over my insecurities.

Oh Lord, I'm so thankful that you are a perfect parent, even when I am not. Thank you for saving me and covering my sin with your righteousness. I long to be the best mom I can for the children you have entrusted to me—despite my insecurities, the countless unknowns, and the ever-changing seasons. Help me to be the mom that you know my children need. And when I fall short, thank you that your grace is sufficient and greater than any mistake I may make.

Grow in me a love for you and your word, even when countless other things are competing for my time, energy, and attention. When I am weary, fill me with your strength. When I'm insecure, remind me that my identity is in you, not in my children or what others think of me. When I sin against my children, give me the humility to ask for their forgiveness and yours. When I am weighed down by guilt that I'm not doing enough or doing it well enough, give me the wisdom to know whether that's your Spirit's conviction or the lies of the enemy. Above all, help me remember that Jesus lived the perfect life on my behalf and that I can rest in that.

Today, I lay my children before you and surrender the good and the hard, the joys and sorrows, and the countless unknowns that cause me to toss and turn at night. Grow in me a love for you that reflects your love to my children each and every day. And by your grace, draw their hearts to you—saving and shaping them, and molding them into your image.

May I always be a conduit of that grace. And thank you that today, you will go on giving more grace.

A Conduit of His Grace

Mouths to feed
And memories to make
Tears to dry
And hearts to shape.

Decisions to guide
Broken hearts to mend
Messes to clean
And a hand to lend.

Hurtful words to absorb
Unconditional love to give
Striving to offer our best
Yet imperfectly we live.

Though failures are often
And weaknesses are felt
Confess our constant need
His strength to be dealt.

They don't need perfection
But our presence and embrace
Pointing to the Savior
A conduit of His grace.

As I shape my children
He is shaping me
Working through my weakness
So only Him, they see.

Trusting Him who loves them
The One who holds their lot
Shaping their little hearts
In ways that I cannot.

The calling of a mother
Is to lay herself down
Carrying a cross
That leads to a crown.

Journal

SEVENTEEN

Eyes to See Glimpses of Grace

"Continue steadfastly in prayer, being watchful in it with thanksgiving."

COLOSSIANS 4:2

GRACE IN A LINE

God is pouring out his grace to us today—
I just need to notice it!

It had been one of those weeks. You know the kind—a week when challenges, disappointments, and stress seem to come from every angle. This particular week, my chronic pain had flared, one of my kids was having difficulties at school, financial stress was hanging on me like a dead weight, and I was feeling like a failure as a mom, discouraged by the uptick in bickering and challenging behaviors.

"Mom guilt" had a death grip on me. "I'm clearly doing something wrong and falling short of the mom I need to be," I groaned.

Trying to fight back tears as I started to fix food for everyone, I aimlessly searched the refrigerator, hoping my kids wouldn't notice I was trying not to cry and ask me what the matter was. But when I spotted the week-old leftovers now looking more like a science experiment than a meal, the dam finally broke, and the tears ran down my cheeks.

My boys noticed I was upset and asked if I was okay. I tried to downplay it. "I'm just having a hard day," I told them. I knew I couldn't be fully honest, since one of them had contributed in large part to how I was feeling.

But, despite my best attempts, they were unconvinced. "Mom," one of them said, "you do so much for us and never do anything for yourself. You're always sacrificing for us, all while not feeling well. Come on, we're going to take care of you." They ran upstairs and came back down with a massage bean-bag chair and a toy foot spa belonging to one of my daughters. My older son ordered a coffee to be delivered to the house and escorted me to the place they had set up for me to be "pampered." I was so struck by their compassion and thoughtfulness that I stopped resisting and did as they asked.

For the next hour, my boys set aside everything to take turns rubbing my shoulders, pampering me with a toy foot spa (which worked surprisingly well!) and encouraging my weary heart by sharing why they were thankful that I'm their mom.

That day, God used the children I was convinced I was failing to be the hands and feet of Christ to me. (And I feel I ought to add here: our house does not always *quite* reach these heights of thoughtful selflessness.) As I sat being pampered, I sensed the Spirit say, *Sarah, I see you, and I'm using your own children and your sense of failure as a mom to remind you that it's not all up to you. I'm at work in your children in ways you can't always see, and I'm at work not because you're a perfect mom but because I am greater than your failures, weaknesses, and limitations. And just like your children, I am here to comfort you and provide for you in your weariness.*

Friend, I don't know about you, but I find it far easier to grow discouraged by the areas where I'm falling short as a mom than to notice areas of growth and glimpses of grace, and far easier to notice future challenges and daily difficulties than answered prayers and daily blessings.

I imagine I'm not the only one. Most of motherhood is a process of two steps forward and one step back. Just as we start to figure out one season, we enter a new, unfamiliar one. A child starts to show growth in one area only for a new area of struggle to test our patience with them. We empty laundry baskets, only to find them overflowing with dirty clothes two days later. There are not many aspects of motherhood that have a clear start and finish, or any measurable success. Change, growth, and forward progress can be so slow that we can miss it altogether if we don't take the time to stop and look for it. And as a result, we can find ourselves easily discouraged and missing the many blessings right in front of us.

I'm learning (albeit slowly) that the greatest way to counteract a spirit of discouragement and weariness is to look for evidence of God's grace—in my children, in myself, and in the circumstances around me. This is what it means to "continue steadfastly in prayer, being watchful in it with thanksgiving."

If we're only focused on the work still to be done and prayers yet to be answered in the way we're hoping or expecting, we will miss the countless "little" answers to prayer and unexpected blessings along the way. On the other hand, looking for ways in which we see God's faithfulness and grace at work right in front of us leads to a sense of joy, a greater prayerfulness, and a heart of gratitude. So here are few practical ways to consider being "watchful ... with thanksgiving."

IN MY CHILDREN

Ask yourself: Where do I see growth in my child(ren)? What struggle did we use to deal with but haven't had to address in a while? In what ways have challenges provided an opportunity to share the gospel with them? How have I seen my children show me grace and forgiveness when I've sinned against them? What encouraging and Christ-honoring characteristics do I see in my kids that are because of God's grace and not my own doing?

You may see loads of ways in which you desire your children to grow. But focus on positive answers for a moment. You will find encouragement when you stop and look for growth and evidence of God's work in your kids—even if only by inches!

IN MYSELF

Ask yourself: Where have I seen growth in my own life? Are there areas of sin or struggle that don't have as much of a grip on me as they once did? When I've been weary, discouraged, or lonely, how has God shown me his presence and comfort? Is there a friend that God has placed in my life as an encouragement and support? What areas has God gifted me in, which I can be thankful for?

You will always have areas in which you desire to grow, and you will always be met with new challenges and seasons to navigate. But if you take the time to notice and show gratitude for God's tangible grace, love, and provision for you, you will be better able to find joy in the journey of motherhood, rather than being fixated on how far you fall short of where you want to be.

IN CIRCUMSTANCES

When you're having a hard day but are stopped in your tracks by a breathtaking sunset, remind yourself that the God who paints the colors of the sky is the same God who rules over every little detail of your life. He is reminding you of his glory, goodness, and presence in that moment.

When you feel you're falling short of being the mom you want to be, but then your child walks in and hands you a gift they've made or some flowers they've picked, stop and enjoy the love of your heavenly Father being shown through your child.

When you're spread thin after a long week and a friend randomly asks if she can bring you dinner, soak in the care of your heavenly Father, who sees and meets you in tangible ways.

When your plans are ruined by sickness or a cancellation, but your unexpected downtime ends up providing an opportunity for your family to connect during a busy season, be ready to see that God's grace can redeem disappointments for his good purposes.

Sister, motherhood is wonderful and hard all at the same time. Too often, we can be our own worst enemy, fixating on where we're falling short and glossing over the multitude of ways in which God has been and is being faithful. In his kindness, the Holy Spirit can open our eyes to see his tangible and present care for us—yes, sometimes even through the precious children he has entrusted to us. Today, take the time to look around and see the blessings and glimpses of God's grace all around you. You just might be surprised at how much you have to be grateful for.

REFLECT

- ~ In what ways have you seen glimpses of God's grace to you or your children lately?

- ~ Are there areas where you see growth in yourself or your children, which you can thank God for today?

Journal

EIGHTEEN

God's Grace Through the Local Church

*"And let us consider how to stir up one another to love
and good works, not neglecting to meet together, as is the
habit of some, but encouraging one another, and all the
more as you see the Day drawing near."*

HEBREWS 10:24-25

GRACE IN A LINE

My church is God's gift to me, and it's good to look to
God's people for help and encouragement.

I was a new bride when we relocated to another state, far
from my family and friends. Within a year I became a
mother. It was a difficult pregnancy and required a longer
than normal recovery.

It had been a hard and lonely year, but when my child was
a year old, I decided to attend a women's Bible study at our
local church. Afterwards, as I was walking out, another mom
caught up to me and introduced herself. I must have had
"lonely" written all over my face because she invited me, right
then and there, to come to her house for lunch. Clearing off
her kitchen table, she threw together some tuna sandwiches

which she served on paper plates. While our children played with toys nearby, she prayed with me. Through her words of gospel truth and grace, and through her humble hospitality and genuine care, she broke through the hopeless sense of loneliness I had been feeling.

This was the local church doing what the local church is called to do—believers living in community and serving as instruments of grace in one another's lives.

The church is God's gift to us as we travel this hard life on our way to our eternal home. Church is a place where we can, week by week, meet other moms in our season of life to walk with; where we can get to know mothers at the next stage up who we can lean on for advice; and where we can be encouraged by older moms who have raised children and have the perspective of more years.

That all sounds great. But church doesn't always feel like a gift to a mom.

CHILDREN CHANGE CHURCH

There is no doubt that getting to church is harder when you have children. Once, we so easily got out of the house, enjoyed a peaceful drive to church, were able to worship without interruption, and then enjoyed uninterrupted fellowship with others. Children change all that!

How well I remember getting our children all ready to get into the car when the unpleasant odor of a full diaper or the onset of a toddler tantrum delayed us. One of my sons struggled with separation anxiety, which meant that for many months I spent more time in the nursery than in the service. Exhaustion, postpartum depression, and wiggly children are just some of the things that mark many moms' lives in the early years. This is a season for patience and remembering that "this too shall pass."

As children grow older, busy schedules, late nights out, sports commitments and so on can create pressure to skip church. This is a season to firm up family priorities.

With the teen years can come insecurities with friends and a desire to fit in, which might bring more resistance to attending church. This is a season for prayer and perseverance.

It's wise to be aware of how we might be tempted to compromise our commitment to church as moms:

- *Doing church at home.* Today, with church services now accessible by livestream, the temptation to stay home and do church in our sweats with a cup of coffee can so easily pull us away from being consistently physically present at church on Sundays. The writer of Hebrews reminds us that the Christian life is not a solo race, and so we must not give up on actually meeting together (as much as we are physically able to). We need the church, and the church needs us.

- *Isolation.* Moms who struggle with winter blues, chronic illness, or parenting a child with special needs or health issues can be tempted to withdraw from others. Yet times when we feel least like making an effort to be with others are often when we need that the most—and God has lovingly provided his people to love us with his truth and grace (albeit imperfectly).

- *In and out.* Of course sometimes it's unavoidable, but we can end up habitually showing up to church late and leaving early. This is better than not going at all, but it is hard to experience the ways in which God desires to bless and encourage us through his people if we are fitting church in rather than fitting other things around church.

So, once you have kids, church gets harder, and the temptations are new. All of us will need reminding from time to time why it is worth all the effort.

THE BLESSING OF THE BODY OF CHRIST

In church God, in his kindness, gives others the opportunity to minister to you. While it takes courage and humility to let others know when you're hurting or struggling, God calls his people to love and serve one another and, sometimes, that "other" is us.

In the same way that watching suffering saints praise God through their tears can encourage your faith and increase your resolve to persevere, just by being there you will be an encouragement to others who likely know what it took for you to simply get out the door and to church with small children in tow.

As you allow older mature saints to love and encourage you, your friendship and faith will be an encouragement to them as well. The church becomes stronger when each generation seeks to love the others with the grace God has given.

Whether you are struggling or thriving, you can always contribute to church, even as you lean on the church yourself. You can both give and be a recipient of the "one-anothering" that God calls his people to:

- "Therefore welcome one another as Christ has welcomed you, for the glory of God" (Romans 15:7). As God welcomed us when we were still sinners, we have the joy of showing the love of Christ to those who need it most. Who might need a smile from you or some tuna sandwiches on paper plates?

- God graciously equips "the saints for the work of ministry, for building up the body of Christ" (Ephesians 4:12). What abilities, gifts, and opportunities has God put in your hands to use for the good of his people?

- As we pray for one another, we have the privilege of lifting each other's burdens to the Lord, who is able to do far more than we ask or imagine (Ephesians 3:20, NIV).

I am so thankful that God doesn't save us and then expect us to do life alone. The church offers something the world cannot provide. God, in his grace, gathers people from all generations, from different walks of life, with various gifts, abilities, and experiences, and unites us in our love for Christ and one another. Yes, the church is imperfect, and we will not always live up to our calling as believers. Yes, when we have kids, it would sometimes be easier not to go. Yes, there may be circumstances that prevent you from attending in person from time to time (illness, special-needs difficulties, and so on). But in a world permeated with division, hate, rage, anger, and restlessness, God's people are a light in the darkness.

And along with that, as moms we are given the joyful privilege of exposing our children to the light that's reflected through the community of believers. So next time you are struggling to get children into the car, to keep their attention where it should be during the service, or to bear with childish behavior, pray—pray that they will be drawn to the light themselves and, one day, go out bearing the light of Christ to the world.

Jesus loves your church enough to have given his life for them. Your church is his gracious gift to you. What a privilege and joy he has given us to be instruments of grace to both his chosen people and our own children! The church needs real moms, and real moms need the local church in all their beauty and imperfection.

REFLECT

- What tempts you to make church attendance a lower priority in the season you are currently in?

- How does seeing the church as God's gift to you (and to your children) motivate you to be present (whenever possible) so you can both bless others and be encouraged by them?

Journal

NINETEEN

Trusting our Shepherd in the Darkness

"Even though I walk through the valley of the shadow of death, I will fear no evil, for you are with me; your rod and your staff, they comfort me."

PSALM 23:4-5

GRACE IN A LINE

Jesus is with me and guiding me, however hard the path is.

As we drove away, I glanced back to catch one last glimpse of our teenaged son as his figure faded into the distance. For two months we had waited for this day to come, knowing that him spending an indeterminate number of months at a residential program, hours from home, was the best way for our sweet boy to get the help and healing that we could not provide. But it was still one of the worst decisions a parent has to make. Not knowing how long it would be before we'd see him again, I felt as though someone had ripped out a piece of my heart.

In the lead-up to the day, I had been sure that, once we'd dropped him off, the tears would erupt after months of holding them in. But my eyes were as dry as the Colorado air around me. All I could do was stare out of the window at the passing trees in silence. I was numb: not because I didn't care but because the anguish felt so unbearable that I could feel nothing at all.

Dusk began to fall as we drove through the mountain pass, and I could have sworn the mountain walls on either side of us were slowly closing in. In that moment, it was as if both my heart and my surroundings were leading me straight into the valley of the shadow of death. All I could see was an inch in front of me. Beyond it was pitch blackness and the terror of the unknown. And then… some old familiar words echoed in my mind:

*"Even though I walk through the valley of the shadow
of death,
I will fear no evil,
for you are with me;
your rod and your staff,
they comfort me." (Psalm 23:4-5)*

The words washed over me. I wanted to believe them with all my being. But the numbness felt impenetrable.

"Lord, I don't know if I can do this," I prayed. "How much can a mother's heart endure before it completely shatters? We've prayed—no, we've pleaded—for his healing for more than a decade. We've given everything within us to fight for him, and we've pressed on in the hope of finding healing for our little boy, who has endured so much. Yet, here we are—the very place we'd worked so hard to avoid. The future feels bleak, the unknowns feel endless, my son is hours away from me, and my tattered heart is hanging on by a thread."

*"Even though I walk through the valley of the shadow
of death,
I will fear no evil,
for you are with me;
your rod and your staff,
they comfort me."*

Slowly the words began to spark a faint sense of comfort. Jesus didn't say he would spare me from the valley of the shadow of death. He did say that I need not fear because he is with me in it, guiding and comforting me when I can't see one step in front of me.

I grasped onto this promise with everything I had. I didn't know how the days and weeks and months ahead would look, but he was with me in the valley at that moment. Every breath, every ache in my gut, every fearful thought—he was right there with me. All I could do was cling to his presence and rest in his promise that wherever this valley might lead, he would walk beside me every step of the way.

THE LIGHT WILL DAWN

The months that followed were some of the most excruciating I've endured in my life, but I can tell you that Christ was with my husband and me each step of the way. He nudged us to keep going when we wanted to just sit and wallow in misery; he gave us the strength and guidance we needed when we felt too paralyzed to make a decision; and some days, when the dam of tears finally did break, it was as if he just sat with us in our heartache and grief, comforting us with his presence.

The day finally came when the darkness of the valley began to lift and we saw a faint light begin to dawn on the horizon. But by the time it did, I had seen and experienced the tangible presence and comfort of Jesus in ways like never before. And while we were fighting for faith and hope in the darkness, unbeknown to us, God was doing a powerful work within our child's heart and mind. It's a season I don't ever want to have to endure again, but it's also been a season that's shown me the gentleness of Jesus in our pain and the power of God to work miracles in some of the darkest and most unlikely places.

Sister, as moms we will experience some intensity or length of the valley of the shadow of death. We may have to watch our child endure heartache that we're helpless to do anything about. We may have a dream or expectation of motherhood that comes to a screeching halt with a life-altering diagnosis for ourselves, our husband, or our child. We may endure the anguish of looking at an ultrasound scan, only to see the lifeless form of a precious child when only days before we were daydreaming of what was to come with each little heartbeat. We might toss and turn at night as we grieve a child's choice to reject Christ and our attempts to speak into their life.

Few are the mothers who do not have to walk the dark valley at some time or for the whole time.

And yet… whatever deep sorrows that dark valley may contain for us, we have a Savior who not only walks with us through it but gently leads us with compassion, comfort, and strength. It's in some of the darkest valleys that we'll experience some of the most profound reassurances of Christ's loving care. And when we reach the other side, by God's grace, we will be profoundly different people.

Today, as I reflect back on this uniquely painful season with our child, I still do not know the end of the story. But I do know that my son and I are under the everlasting arms of our good Shepherd. And if you are a child of God, you are too, my friend.

Whatever you, your family, or your child may be enduring today, may these words lead your heart to rest in the peace, comfort, and presence of Christ:

"The LORD is my shepherd; I shall not want.
  He makes me lie down in green pastures.
 He leads me beside still waters.
  He restores my soul.
 He leads me in paths of righteousness
  for his name's sake.

"Even though I walk through the valley of the shadow
 of death,
  I will fear no evil,
 for you are with me;
  your rod and your staff,
  they comfort me.

"You prepare a table before me
  in the presence of my enemies;
 you anoint my head with oil;
  my cup overflows.

"Surely goodness and mercy shall follow me
  all the days of my life,
 and I shall dwell in the house of the LORD
  forever." (Psalm 23)

REFLECT

- ~ Have you experienced a season of walking through the "valley of the shadow of death"? How have you experienced the presence of Jesus in that season?

- ~ If you're there right now, what difference will it make to cling to the knowledge that Jesus will be enough for you today, even as you long for the light to dawn again?

Journal

TWENTY

Finding and Enjoying Your Mom-Strengths

"I praise you, for I am fearfully and wonderfully made.
Wonderful are your works; my soul knows it very well."

PSALM 139:14

GRACE IN A LINE

God made me as me, giving me particular strengths that
I can use in my mothering.

My mom and I used to have a tumultuous relationship. During my high-school years, our differences in personality and perspective (as well as my immaturity) caused a deeply painful season in our relationship. During one of my exasperated outbursts, I cried out, *"I never want to be like you!"*

Now that I'm a mom, I know the pain those words must have inflicted on her. But by God's grace, that wasn't the end of our story. After a few painful years, God grabbed hold of my heart, and he began to restore and heal our relationship. However, as much as I can now say that my mom is a woman I greatly admire and I want to be more like, we are still wired differently. My teenage self was irritated that she wasn't more like me. My young-mom self was insecure because I wasn't more like her. Now, I see that I can appreciate our differences and celebrate both her strengths and mine.

UNIQUELY WIRED

My mom is a naturally structured, self-disciplined, rule-following, organized, type A personality. I, on the other hand, have always been bent toward going with the flow, being less structured and more introspective and highly sensitive to the world around me. If I'm being honest, before the Holy Spirit started his work in my life, rules seemed more like suggestions than obligations (which is why I jokingly say that I've been a great sanctifying tool in my parents' lives!).

Now, as I navigate my own motherhood journey, I've often wished I were more like my mom, so that cleaning and organizing closets invigorated me rather than paralyzed me and so that charts and structured plans were successfully created and followed through on, rather than leaving me overwhelmed.

Recently, I shared with my mom my feelings of guilt about not having more of her strengths. She said something I will never forget: "Sarah, God made you and me different, with different personalities, perspectives, strengths, circumstances—and children. Use the strengths he's given you, rather than getting caught up in trying to fit into another mold. God knew what he was doing when he made you the mother of your children. The very things you perceive as weaknesses are actually strengths that God has given you for your unique calling and family. You can learn from what other moms find helpful, and you can pray for God to grow you in areas of weakness, but tap into the strengths of your unique temperament and ask God to use those to teach, train, and love your children well."

That wisdom has been life-giving for me, and I pray it will be for you as well because, just as our children are uniquely wired, we too are "fearfully and wonderfully made"—and that includes how our various personalities have been crafted by our Creator. We can say, "Wonderful are your works; my soul knows it very well" (Psalm 139:14). God doesn't make mistakes.

JESUS SAW VALUE IN VARIETY

Jesus chose twelve disciples each of whose temperament, strengths, and background were unique. Peter had a strong personality—at times for the better, at times for the worse. God used that quality to form him into a leader who would boldly share the gospel. James and John were passionate brothers, nicknamed "Sons of Thunder" (Mark 3:17). Matthew, the tax collector, appeared to be a detail-oriented disciple with a checkered past. God used him nonetheless. God called each of them to become more like Jesus in their character, but he did not ask them to abandon their individual personalities.

Similarly, we're called to disciple our children using the distinctive strengths, experience, and wisdom that God has given us.

But there's a caveat. The very things that can be strengths can also become weaknesses when they aren't surrendered to Christ. All of our personality traits are God-given, but in our sin we can use each to rebel against him. So, it's worth thinking about what you're like and working through how your particular makeup can be used in a Christ-like way, and how it can be used in the opposite way.

For example, are you a naturally structured person? That can lend itself toward keeping a well-ordered home and motivating your children with a chart that tracks their chores. God is a God of order, and such order can be a reflection of his character to our children (1 Corinthians 14:33, NIV).

Yet a desire for structure can also lead to an unhealthy need for control and the subconscious belief that you have more power over your circumstances than you really do. Your plans and desire for order must be submitted to the sovereignty of God. Make wise plans, but find your rest and confidence in Christ and his wisdom, not in your own sense of being in control.

On the flip side, you may be more like me, preferring to dance in the kitchen with your kids than to organize a closet or draw up a detailed structure for the day. This enables you to easily adapt to the ebbs and flows of an unpredictable life. You are more naturally going to be able to live in the moment, find joy in the unexpected, and not lose your temper when plans go awry. God is a God of joy, creativity, and grace, and when we have the eyes to embrace moments like those, we too reflect the character of God (Psalm 16:11).

Yet a lack of structure can also result in failing to plan ahead when that's needed, lack of order and organization in the home, and lack of the consistency that is helpful for children. Enjoy the moment and give thanks that you can submit to God's plans, but be willing to establish order and structure at the right time and in a balanced way.

Whether you're naturally bent toward optimism or realism, to being driven or laid-back, or to approaching life as a dreamer or pragmatist, there are countless traits that will shape how you parent differently than others, and each is simultaneously a great strength and a potential weakness. Whether it be through a structure that helps us accomplish tasks or through setting aside our to-do list to simply get on the floor to laugh and play with our child, all can be done to the glory of God and for the good of our children. Wisdom looks like knowing which is the time for which.

So stop for a moment and consider: What am I naturally like? How are those things strengths? How could they be weaknesses? Then take a moment to thank God for the unique personality he's given you and ask him to show you both how to wield it as a strength in his service and how you could be tempted to indulge it in a way that's selfish.

CHRIST-LIKE, NOT OTHERS-LIKE

Regardless of our personality, strengths, and style of motherhood, our ultimate goal as disciples who happen to be moms is to grow in Christlikeness. And our ultimate goal in our homes is to lead our children to do the same.

Next time you feel that tinge of guilt come over you when you see another mom parenting differently than you, stop and ask yourself if the Lord is revealing to you something that you do need to repent of and to ask him to change in you. But remember that the answer may very well be "no"—that it may be that she is simply a different mom, parenting differently because she's different, with different kids and circumstances.

Remember, God made you as you, with your personality. This is his gift to you. You don't need to be someone else— just you, using your God-given strengths, reining in your weaknesses, and loving your kids. If those are your aims, then Christ will be glorified, and you will find freedom to be the mom he created you to be.

REFLECT

- Is there another mom you tend to compare yourself to? If so, why?

- What strengths and individual qualities do you see in yourself (personality, gifts, interests, perspective, etc)?

- How might the strengths and qualities you've been given be used to parent your children, even as you seek to grow in areas of weakness?

Journal

TWENTY-ONE

Embrace the Season You're In

*"To everything there is a season, and a time for
every matter under heaven."*

ECCLESIASTES 3:1

GRACE IN A LINE

This season of motherhood is a gift, that can be enjoyed
instead of wished away.

I was slowly navigating my way through the grocery store
for the first time with my newborn son when an older
woman came over and began cooing over him. Suddenly,
she looked up and offered these unsolicited words: "Enjoy
this season, honey! Little children, little problems—big
children, BIG problems!"

And with that, she walked away.

That is a daunting warning! And (thankfully) it's simply not biblical. Every season of life brings joys to cherish, lessons to learn, loved ones to nurture, and sorrows to grieve over—whether we have children or not. Wonderfully, God promises to give us grace according to our every need right when we need it. His grace is not only sufficient for us, but Christ's power is made perfect in our weakness (2 Corinthians 12:9).

As I look back on my years of parenting, I thank God for every season of raising children. As it turns out, while I was in the midst of learning to parent, the Lord was patiently parenting and sanctifying me! From sleepless nights with newborns to sleepless nights when teens were out late with the car, God taught me important lessons of trust, forgiveness, serving, and contentment. I needed every lesson he taught through the parenting years (and that he continues to teach—you don't stop being a parent when your children leave home!). And while there has certainly been a measure of suffering along the way, the joys have far outweighed the sorrows.

Paul said, "I have *learned* in whatever situation I am to be content" (Philippians 4:11, emphasis added). I find it very encouraging to know that contentment was something that even the great apostle had to learn. God wants us, too, to learn to trust and depend upon him day by day—neither dreading nor longing for the days yet to come in this life. The truth is that he has many blessings to give when we accept with gratitude the season that we're in, even the more difficult ones.

So, here is my simple encouragement to you right now: embrace the season you're in.

God gives us eyes to see the good gifts he has given. At every stage of life, he teaches us important truths about our need and his faithfulness. And he warns us neither to romanticize the past nor fantasize about the future. Our temptation is to believe life will be better and things will be easier when the kids are through a particularly difficult stage, or to wish we could go back to earlier days when our children were young or still living at home.

Not long ago, I sat next to a young mom who has an 18-month-old and a 3-month-old and who was understandably exhausted! As she nursed her baby and we chatted, she shared, "I had a hard time getting pregnant, and I'm so thankful for my children. But I didn't know it would be this exhausting, and it makes me wonder why I was not more content in the season before we had kids."

It is better to be content in each season than to wish we'd been content as we look back on every season.

Godly wisdom teaches us both to be honest about the challenges of the present and to find contentment in the particular blessings and joys of the present. Ecclesiastes 3:12-13 reminds us that "to be joyful and to do good as long as [we] live ... [to] eat and drink and take pleasure in all [our] toil—this is God's gift to man."

As we learn to embrace the hard things along with the good things, we will not only be able to delight in the diversity of every season, we'll be more inclined to benefit from God's good purposes in refining and growing us.

So, ask God to open your eyes to see the blessings and opportunities right where you are because every season is a good season in the eyes of the Lord!

With God's help, we can learn to love the season we're in...

Early childhood provides the joy of experiencing the wonders of God's creation through the eyes of our children as they take delight in things we have come to take for granted. During these years, we are given the privilege of teaching the very basics of life: how to walk and talk, first lessons in getting along with others, the rewards of obedience, and learning to be responsible. While these can be physically exhausting years, they are also filled with precious moments: little hands tucked in ours, hearts of unwavering trust in our love, calming fears about monsters under the bed.

The childhood years of 6-12 are less physically exhausting. They offer valuable opportunities to teach and model important gospel truths to moldable hearts. These are the years of creating fun family memories that can build a foundation of security and love which will help our children navigate their way through their teens on the way to adulthood. During these years we have a captive audience in our children! Free from diapers and nap times but not yet dealing with the pull of peer pressure or the desire for independence, we can enjoy family outings, work on projects together, and help our children discover some of the good gifts God has given them as they try new things.

The teen years allow emerging adults to test their wings while still under our protection and influence. Although it's true that some teens push their limits further than they should (or, perhaps, simply further than we are comfortable with), it's a wonderful season of preparation before they leave home to make their own way into the world. Young people have opportunities to discover their gifts and abilities, and we get to cheer them on in their successes and comfort them when life smacks them in the face. We begin to transition from being our child's primary authority to providing godly counsel and correction when needed. It is also a time when there tend to be many moments that prompt our prayer life to grow more vibrant!

The emptying nest: For some, this season can be the most difficult of all, yet of course in a sense it's the culmination of all those previous seasons of parenting. Our goal as a parent is to work ourselves out of a job. When our children leave home as (hopefully) responsible adults, we may miss their daily presence, but we can celebrate the work God has done in all of our lives. And, in God's kindness, over time we may discover that the children we have launched into the world have become our very dearest friends.

By God's grace, while I have loved and grown through each phase of parenting, at the end of each season I always thought that the most recent one was the best season—even when it was paved with parenting potholes and ditches of humility along the way. It's often only as we look back that we can see the faithfulness of God, who has provided strength in our weakness.

Sister, embrace the season you're in, for every moment is holy when we parent for the glory of God.

REFLECT

- What season are you in right now? What's great about it? What challenges come with it?

- Where have you seen God's faithfulness even in the hardest days?

- When are you most tempted to believe past days were better or that things will be easier in the future? What will you thank God for, right now?

Journal

TWENTY-TWO

Childishness Is Not Disobedience

*"Let the children come to me, and do not hinder them, for
to such belongs the kingdom of God."*

LUKE 18:16

GRACE IN A LINE

I can be gentle with childish behavior,
just as God is gentle with me.

I can still feel the embarrassing sting of my high-school
basketball coach screaming my name in front of a packed
crowd of students and parents. For reasons no one could
understand, he had it in for me. I became paralyzed by the
fear of being the target of his anger, and, eventually, I started
living up to the failure that he seemed to expect of me,
convinced I couldn't do anything right in his eyes.

What he failed to realize was that the fear of his intimida-
tion and shaming words were never going to bring out the
best in me. Had he encouraged me in my strengths instead
and used moments of failure as teaching moments rather
than attacking me as a person, he would have motivated me
to grow, develop, and thrive under his leadership. Instead,

I was left with some emotional scars that have not easily healed.

We're moms, not basketball coaches. But frustrating moments in motherhood can tempt us to respond to our children in a similar way to how my coach responded to me. You have the power to encourage and teach your children in response to their childish mistakes, and you have the power to react in anger or irritation over them acting like, well, children. Sadly, I've seen my own tendency to respond in an all-too-similar way to my coach.

BUTTON-PUSHING IS NOT SIN

It is a fact that we should expect that our kids will sin. But there's another aspect of childhood that has a tendency to push our buttons—and that's their childishness. From the moment our children can crawl (or even before), we're confronted by their childish actions: choices that aren't outright disobedient or sinful, but rather are the result of a child who is still developing and learning to think before they act.

I'm sure we could swap countless stories about childish and impulsive decisions that ended in a ball going through the window when a child decided that throwing a ball near the house was a good idea, or in flour exploding all over us when a child squeezed the package out of pure curiosity, or in us grimacing in pain after a little one decided "Now is a good time to run and jump on mom's lap" despite there being a piping-hot cup of coffee in our hands. Sometimes those moments leave us scratching our heads and wondering, "What in the world would possess my child to do such a thing?" At other times, they push our last button and cause us to react in anger and exasperation over childish actions that have caused inconvenience, mess, and unforeseen consequences. Whether they are two or 20, our children will make mistakes and poor decisions from time to time simply as a part of their learning, growing, and maturing.

THE HEART BEHIND THE ACTION

When these moments come, we have a choice: to respond out of frustration over the action and its consequences or respond to the heart behind the action.

Here's one example. A few years back, one of my kids ran into the room and jumped on my lap, causing my hot cup of coffee to spill on my legs and the surrounding carpet. "Owwwww!" I yelled, involuntarily. But as the initial shock passed and I saw the look of horror, fear, and embarrassment on my child's face, I realized I had a choice. Believe me, it was sure tempting to yell, "Why in the world would you do that? Can't you see I had a coffee in my hands?!"

But thankfully, the words didn't make it from my brain to my mouth before the Lord gave me insight to recognize that underneath her impulsive actions, which had caused pain and a mess was a desire to show me love. She wasn't trying to be hurtful, and she wasn't being disobedient. She was simply still in the process of learning to be aware of her surroundings before acting. So instead of focusing purely on the outcome of her actions, I tried to rein in my frustration over the mess and take the time to tell her how much I loved it when she wanted to climb on my lap and give me hugs, but that she also needed to learn to observe what's happening before simply acting. She helped me clean up the coffee and said how sorry she was that she hurt me. Instead of her feeling ashamed and beaten down (as I often felt by my coach), she was able to learn from what had happened and inch one step closer to maturity, still assured of my love.

I haven't always responded graciously to my kids being childish. But the Holy Spirit has been convicting me in these moments, causing me to stop and consider, "What if God treated me this way? What if he heaped shame on me every time I accidentally broke a special heirloom, caused my child to miss out on an opportunity because I forgot about the sign-up deadline, or received a speeding ticket when my distracted mind missed the speed-limit sign?" I'd feel the sting of natural consequences—something that is broken and cannot be replaced, a disappointed child, and a speeding ticket to pay for. But if the Lord looked at me in those moments with a look of accusation, disappointment, and harshness, I would not feel the love of the Father, who is for me and filled with grace toward me. God would be a figure I was only ever one step from making frustrated or angry with me.

God is not like that. He understands that we're human, and he is compassionate when we make a mistake. Similarly, motherhood provides constant opportunities to get down to our children's level and respond to their mistakes in a way that shows them that they themselves are more important to us than the mess they made or how their choices reflect upon us.

But to do that, we first need to know what a childish action is and isn't. I've found it helpful, in those moments, to consider a few diagnostic questions before responding.

1. Is my child disobeying a command I've given them?

2. Are they clearly sinning in some other way?

3. Has my child caused inconvenience to me, and might I be tempted to confuse that consequence with actual sin?

If the answer to either of the first two questions is yes, then we should address what has happened with loving discipline. However, if the answers are no and no, then most likely this was childishness, and instead of discipline, we can take the time to walk our child through what they were thinking, why that choice wasn't good, and how they can make a better choice next time. Often, the learning comes from thinking it through and then helping clean up the mess.

REMEMBER YOUR OWN NEED FOR GRACE

Friend, if you're reading this and thinking, "I have so often reacted out of emotion and with harshness when my kids have made childish mistakes," let me encourage you with James 4:6: "But he gives more grace." Not only is God able to forgive and help you grow in this area, but each day is filled with new mercies and fresh opportunities. With the Lord's help, you can grow in this area, just as you're trying to help your children learn and grow. And when you do react in the wrong way (which will inevitably happen from time to time), you can use those moments as opportunities to ask for your children's forgiveness and God's forgiveness, and show them how you, too, need grace and forgiveness.

So, ask the Lord to give you wisdom, insight, and patience to distinguish between disobedient and childish actions, and to respond accordingly. Because when you do, these occasions become fertile ground for your children to grow and flourish in wisdom and maturity. That is gospel grace.

REFLECT

- ~ How would you describe the difference between childishness and disobedience? Consider making a list of what would fall under the "childishness" category and what would fall under the "disobedience" category to give yourself a helpful framework for how to best respond to different scenarios.

Journal

TWENTY-THREE

Grace for the Mom Raising a Child with Extra Needs

*"But God chose what is foolish in the world to shame the wise;
God chose what is weak in the world to shame the strong."*

1 CORINTHIANS 1:27

GRACE IN A LINE

When parenting is at its most challenging, Jesus will most
help me. He will equip me for everything he calls me
to do as a mom.

Every child is a gift. Every. Single. One.
Whether they share our DNA or have come into
our family through adoption, each child is uniquely
made by the same God who created this beautifully complex
world. It has always fascinated me that out of our own four
children, each has unique looks, personality, strengths, weaknesses, and interests. This, in part, is what makes motherhood
so beautifully wonderful and so unbelievably challenging all
at the same time.

But just as everything in this life has been impacted by the effects of living in a sin-cursed world, so will our children be. And for some children, those effects have more evidently impacted their body or mind, adding extra challenges and needs to navigate.

In our family, those extra needs have taken the form of chronic illness in all of our children as well as life-altering neurological and behavioral challenges in one of them. Both of these have impacted nearly every part of family life.

Although all of our children will have various needs and challenges (just as we do), there are some who will require "above and beyond" care, with needs ranging from extreme allergies, learning disabilities, or chronic illness to genetic disabilities, cancer, or neurological disorders. This wide range of situations, including some that most people would describe as "special needs," we will call "extra needs" here, to include any child who has needs above and beyond the normal childhood challenges. Each will have varying degrees of impact, but all add additional layers and challenges to our role as a mom.

If this is your experience, I want to start by saying one thing: you can love your child wholeheartedly and unconditionally and grieve the loss and pain which their extra needs bring. It does not need to be one or the other.

GRIEVE WHAT ISN'T AND MAY NEVER BE
I mention grief first because I have always tended to feel ashamed that I've felt grief about my son's challenges, and ashamed that I feel weary about the constant needs and the impact they have on us.

But a couple of years back, the Lord led me to understand what's called "ambiguous loss"—a kind of loss that educator

Pauline Boss explains as something that "differs from ordinary loss in that there is no verification of death or no certainty that the person will come back or return to the way they used to be" (www.ambiguousloss.com/about/faq/, accessed 4/28/23). In a sense, we feel frozen in our grief, unable to move forward or begin the process of healing because we face our loss (of expectations, hopes, "normality") in a fresh way every day.

I found this profoundly helpful. It suddenly gave validity to my chronic, underlying sense of grief over my child's life-altering needs. Grieving that was not a sign that I loved him less than I should. It was simply a normal response to seeing the profound impact that those challenges were having on him, myself, and others around him. Grief was actually flowing out of my love for him, not in spite of it.

The reality is that, when you're reminded of these challenges on a daily basis but are called to serve and sacrifice for the one who reminds you of what's been lost or never had, grief will be a frequent visitor. We need to give ourselves grace to acknowledge our grief when it comes. But it's equally important to remember that we can bring our grief, confusion, and questions to our God, "the Father of mercies and God of all comfort, who comforts us in all our affliction" (2 Corinthians 1:3-4).

ACCEPT WHAT IS

The painful realities and added challenges that come with a child's special needs can be heartbreaking, but our pain is further multiplied when we get trapped in the cycle of thinking, "If only…" If we allow grumbling and discontentment to take up residence in our hearts, choosing to fixate on what isn't rather than accepting what God has allowed, peace and joy will be strangers to us. I know all too well the temptation to distract myself from my reality or to focus on how things used to be (or how I expected them to be). But if we dwell on the life we desire for ourselves and our child, rather than the life God has chosen, then we miss out on seeing and experiencing the blessings that he has for us right where we are.

Sister, God has called each of us to walk the road he has marked out for us for his good purposes. As hard as our calling may feel at times, the writer of Hebrews spurs us on to "be content with what you have, for [God] has said, 'I will never leave you nor forsake you'" (Hebrews 13:5). We are to be content in all circumstances—even circumstances that may never change this side of heaven.

But that's easier said than done, which is precisely why the promise of God's presence is so precious. He assures us, "I will never leave you nor forsake you." Every morning that you wake up to be met by the difficulties of the day ahead, remember that his grace, comfort, and strength meet you as well—today, tomorrow, and every day after.

The power to be content and at peace as we raise a child with particularly challenging needs lies in the strength and comfort of his presence, not in the hope of better days. And by God's grace, the more we experience his presence, the more we will grow in contentment—not because our pain is gone but because we have the peace of Christ within it.

GOD'S KINGDOM IN AN UPSIDE-DOWN WORLD

"God chose what is foolish in the world to shame the wise; God chose what is weak in the world to shame

the strong; God chose what is low and despised in the
world, even things that are not, to bring to nothing
things that are, so that no human being might boast in
the presence of God." (1 Corinthians 1:27-29)

The world values independence. God values dependence on him. The world values outward beauty. God values the beauty of Christ-like character. The world values pride and success. The Lord values humility and sacrificial love. The world values what we can do for ourselves. God values a faith that rests in what Christ has done on our behalf. The world may see your child as a hindrance, a problem to be fixed, or a life of less value. But Jesus sees your child as a life worth laying down his life for.

You and I have the difficult privilege of watching firsthand how God can use a child whom the world might consider "foolish," "weak," and "low" to impact the lives of those around them in countless ways for God's glory—often through the very challenges which the world perceives as disadvantages. And no matter what lies ahead, we can hold onto the confident hope that if they place their hand in his by faith (or if they don't have the mental capacity to make a conscious spiritual decision), one day our child will be fully free from all that holds their body or mind hostage to the brokenness of this world (Revelation 21:4).

Sister, today, if you are facing a fresh sense of grief over a child with any form of special needs, it's okay to let the tears come, pour out your heart before the Lord, and ask for a renewed sense of his comfort, presence, and strength for what he has called you to. Then remind yourself that God has chosen this hard road with your specific child and circumstances for his good and sovereign purposes. If he's called you to the privilege of caring for a child with extra needs, he's giving you the opportunity to walk in the footsteps of Christ and display the gospel by laying down your life for another, even when they may have nothing to give in return. Press on in the truth that God promises he will never leave you nor forsake you, and that he will give you the grace for whatever lies ahead. As you look to Christ, let your grief over what's been lost increase your longing for what's to come, and let your sense of weakness move you to rely on the grace that God gives you to do what he's calling you to today.

REFLECT

- If you've been given the high calling of raising a child with extra needs, what are some of the doubts, questions, emotions, and challenges that you face on a daily basis?

- Do you allow yourself the freedom to grieve honestly before the Lord (and others you can trust)?

- Amid the many challenges, can you see ways in which God has equipped you, provided for you, and brought unexpected blessings in and through the life of your child?

Journal

TWENTY-FOUR

Grace for Our Fears

"My grace is sufficient for you, for my power is made perfect in weakness."

2 CORINTHIANS 12:9

GRACE IN A LINE

God is in control, and God is good,
and I can trust him with my fears.

My two-year-old had come down with a nasty flu that was causing life-threatening dehydration in babies and toddlers in our area. So when I couldn't get him to take any fluids and he became lifeless, our pediatrician urged us to immediately go to the hospital.

As I sat at the bedside of my sick son, fear pulsing through my veins in rhythm to the IV dripping life-saving fluids into his tiny body, I quietly pleaded with God to heal my child. After the nurse left a few minutes later, I happened to glance down at the clipboard she'd left behind and read, "Mother is very fearful."

What?! Was it that obvious that my heart was anxious? As I continued to pray, the Holy Spirit spoke to my heart: "Fear not, for I am with you ... Fear not, nor be afraid" (Isaiah 43:5; 44:8).

I choked back tears as I realized that God already knew that I was very afraid! I knew his word didn't promise that nothing bad would ever happen, and so, rather than trusting in my son's return to health, I needed to know how to find the peace God promised even in the midst of the storm.

In God's kindness, after three days I brought my son home, fully restored to health. But my questions lingered far longer. The endless (and tormenting) list of frightening possibilities and fears of motherhood drove me to the Lord in prayer. I desperately wanted to be set free from the fears that enslaved me and which the nurse had so easily seen in me.

I am sure that I am not the only Christian who struggles with fear. So the question is: *where do we turn when fear threatens to steal our peace?*

As moms, our greatest fears are often attached to the lives and futures of our children. We watch the evening news or a sad movie through a completely different lens than we once did. When something bad happens close to home, we hug our kids a little tighter and wonder if we should stop letting them walk to school without us. But while God calls us to protect vulnerable children, he doesn't want us (or them) to live in fear, to waste time worrying about things we can't control, or to keep our kids from doing anything that might go wrong. Our primary calling is not to make sure that nothing can ever go wrong by never allowing our kids to do anything that involves risk!

Fear steals our peace when it dominates our thoughts and takes hold of us. During the days following my son's stay in the hospital, my heart was full of questions, such as: How does a mother experience freedom from anxiety? What difference does knowing God make in the middle of the night when fear crowds in? As I wrestled with such questions, Psalm 16 taught me four concrete ways to find freedom from both real and imagined fears.

PUT YOUR HOPE IN GOD ALONE

"Preserve me, O God, for in you I take refuge, I say to the LORD, 'You are my Lord; I have no good apart from you.'" (Psalm 16:1-2)

By nature, our happiness ebbs and flows according to our circumstances. When our children are happy and doing well, we feel happy and content. When finances are secure, our husband loves us well, we have good health, and so on, we don't tend to doubt that God is good and loves us. But when life turns in an unwanted direction through job loss, chronic pain, a rebellious child, an accident, or any other kind of suffering, our response can reveal where we are functionally putting our hope.

God's word helps us recognize the things we may be looking to for peace and happiness—unreliable things that were not designed to bear such weight. It only takes one crisis to reveal that our belief that we are in control is only ever an illusion. Our true and unshakable hope is in knowing that the God who loves us and gave his life for us is always in control. He is all-powerful, always good, and always merciful in all his ways—a firm foundation on which you can confidently stand. Fears will come, but when they do, we can bring them under this truth and no longer give them the power to control us.

He simply asks you to put your hope in him above all other things.

REMIND YOURSELF THROUGHOUT THE DAY THAT THE LORD IS NEAR

"I have set the LORD always before me; because he is at my right hand, I shall not be shaken. Therefore, my heart is glad, and my whole heart rejoices; my flesh also dwells secure." (Psalm 16:8-9)

When God tells his people not to fear, the reason he almost always gives is that he is with us. We enjoy his presence with us through the Holy Spirit. We are not alone in a sea of fears or hardships. We are never on our own.

One day, when Jesus returns again, he will make all things new, and we will live face to face in his presence forever. As we wait for that blessed day, we will find rest by locating our hope in God's promise to be with us moment by moment. Even in the midst of life's disappointments, griefs, and unmet expectations, we can keep a quiet heart by remembering that God is with us and for us. So when waves of fear threaten to steal your peace, quiet your anxious heart by hearing the voice of Jesus say, "Take heart; it is I. Do not be afraid" (Matthew 14:27).

He simply asks you to trust him.

REST IN GOD'S SOVEREIGN WISDOM AND PROVIDENCE

"You hold my lot." (Psalm 16:5)

A significant key to experiencing unwavering peace is resting in God's wise providence and the knowledge that nothing can touch our lives that is not according to his loving purposes for our eternal good and his glory. He holds all that we have and are.

The more we meditate on God's love, mercy, and faithfulness, the more we will trust that he alone knows what is best for us and for those we love, including our precious children. God is working all things together to prepare us for a glorious eternity in his presence that will be beyond anything we can hope or imagine. He directs your every step as you walk toward your eternal home with him.

He simply asks you to remember that "underneath are the everlasting arms" (Deuteronomy 33:27).

FIX YOUR EYES ON FUTURE GRACE

> *"The lines have fallen for me in pleasant places; indeed, I have a beautiful inheritance ... You make known to me the path of life; in your presence there is fullness of joy; at your right hand are pleasures forevermore."*
>
> *(Psalm 16:6, 11)*

Life is hard, and no one escapes suffering in this sin-cursed world. But the greater reality is that God is writing our story into his grand story of redemption, weaving both the good and hard days together for our eternal joy. One day soon, Jesus will return and usher in the kingdom of heaven. On that day, our fears will be swallowed up by rejoicing, and we will worship our Savior for the sacrifice he made on our behalf. All fear banished forever, we will gaze at the unfathomable beauty of Christ and experience joy and gladness beyond anything we have ever imagined!

Your fears, when seen through the lens of faith in his promises of future grace, will seem a lot smaller. So take courage; the things you fear will never have the final word, for they are not the end of the story.

He simply asks you to set your heart on the joy that is yours in Jesus.

It is possible, as daughters of our heavenly Father, to conquer our fears for our children. By the grace of God, it's possible for a nurse to note on her hospital chart, "Mom is amazingly calm and peaceful." As we remember and take hold of these truths from Psalm 16, I can bear witness to God's faithfulness to moms who desire freedom from the grip of fear. He simply asks us to trust his sovereign love and goodness.

REFLECT

Take a moment to look at your own fears.

- What fears for your child are currently causing a turbulent spirit and stealing your joy? What unhelpful responses or decisions could these fears prompt in you?

- Which of these four truths from Psalm 16 do you need to call to mind and base your prayers on?

Journal

TWENTY-FIVE

Through the Cracks

"We have this treasure in jars of clay, to show that the
surpassing power belongs to God and not to us."

2 CORINTHIANS 4:7

GRACE IN A LINE

God loves to work through weakness.
Weakness doesn't define me; it can lead me
to the one who does.

There once was a water carrier who traveled every day with two earthen pots hanging from a pole balanced across her shoulders. One pot was strong and solid; the other had a crack in its side. Whenever the water carrier returned home, the cracked pot was only ever half full. Over time, that pot grew discouraged, ashamed that it couldn't fulfill the job it was meant to. One day, it expressed its shame to the water carrier, telling her it would understand if she wanted to replace it with a pot without cracks.

The water carrier replied, "On our walk home, I want you to look to the side of the road. For too long, you have been looking down, comparing yourself to others and not noticing how you and the crack in your side have brought untold beauty into my life."

So, on the journey home, that pot did as the water carrier had said. To its surprise, along the path there was a dazzling array of beauty, color, and life. The water carrier, in her wisdom, had sprinkled seeds along the path. These seeds were watered every day as a result of the crack in the pot's side, and the path that had once been barren and devoid of life was now resplendent with an array of beautiful wild flowers.

THE CRACKS OF CHRONIC PAIN

I have often felt like this broken earthen pot. Long seasons of chronic physical, mental, and emotional pain have affected every part of my life as a mom, tempting me to believe that these "cracks" have rendered me useless—nothing more than a burden to those I love.

Can you relate?

Some of our cracks are obvious and physically debilitating; others are emotional or mental—unseen limitations that make even the simplest tasks more difficult. The truth is, more of us are carrying these cracks than we're aware of.

Sister, like that pot, you may be keenly aware of the cracks that you wish to be free from. They only seem to slow you down, make you less efficient, and fill your life with insecurity, disappointment, and frustration. And yet this story points to scriptural truths that you and I can find comfort in. Paul encourages us: "We have this treasure in jars of clay, to show that the surpassing power belongs to God and not to us." We live in weak and broken vessels, cracked by the effects of living in a fallen world. But when God works through us despite our weakness, it's obvious that it's due to his power. It's those very cracks that can display the power and presence of Jesus in our lives to those around us—including our children.

There's no sugarcoating how difficult days can be for a mom battling weakness and illness. Yet I have also seen glimpses of God's grace flowing through it to develop character in my children. Although I certainly don't have all the answers, I know that God is at work through my cracks in ways I can't always see. And I have no doubt that he is at work through yours as well.

Still, I find it a daily struggle to keep that perspective and not allow the overwhelming feelings of guilt, disappointment, and discouragement to speak louder than the truth. I guess it is the same for you too. So here are a few reminders that have helped me change the negative narrative that I'm prone to listen to.

1. YOUR WEAKNESS: PART OF YOUR CHILDREN'S STORY AS MUCH AS YOURS

When you hear the whispered lie that your children would be better off with a healthy, energetic mom, remember that God can use the struggles you face to be a tool in your children's life for his purposes, even if you can't see how that can be at the moment. God can use disappointments and changed plans to give opportunities for our children to take on greater responsibility, to step up and serve where there's a need, and to grow the skills to face future setbacks. God may be using our lack to show them how God loves and cares for us because of his grace, not because of what we can do for him or others:

> *"His delight is not in the strength of the horse,*
> *nor his pleasure in the legs of a man,*
> *but the LORD takes pleasure in those who fear him,*
> *in those who hope in his steadfast love."*
>
> *(Psalm 147:10-11)*

2. YOU DON'T HAVE TO APPEAR INDESTRUCTIBLE

Too often, I've tried to be a stoic, gritting my teeth through the pain as though I'm a better mom if I never let my limitations have an impact. But it's okay to acknowledge our limits. It's an opportunity to show our kids what it looks like to walk humbly and in dependence on Christ in life's disappointments. At times, pushing through and enduring is lovingly sacrificial, and it gives our children a glimpse of Christ, the Servant-King. At other times, the wise thing to do is listen to our body and ask for help, and that teaches our children that our worth is not found in being independent and indestructible but in dependent faith in Christ (Hebrews 4:15-16). And as the drips of water flow through our painful cracks, it allows our children the opportunity to grow in compassion, be attentive to the needs around them, and learn how to sit with others suffering the discomfort of pain and grief.

3. ALLOW YOUR CHILDREN TO ENTER INTO THE HEALTHY PROCESS OF GRIEF

Rather than simply complaining or having a cynical spirit, we can show our children what it looks like to grieve over disappointments and pain, and wrestle with questions before the Lord in honesty. When we're honest with God, we're in a position to receive his comfort and help (Psalm 73:14-17, 21-26). Allowing our children into this process will serve them well as they grow and are faced with their own griefs and sorrows.

4. LOOK FOR UNEXPECTED GRACES IN UNEXPECTED PLACES

Often, once I surrender and accept what God has allowed in my life as his kind providence, I find an unexpected, sweet peace in that acceptance. More often than not, it's in that place of forced rest and quietness that I experience unexpected, sweet moments with the Lord, and often with my children as well. God can redeem our disappointments and sense of loss if we have the eyes to see it. He promises to be faithful to equip us to be the moms our children need, even if we are riddled with cracks. He assures you and me, "My grace is sufficient for you, for my power is made perfect in weakness" (2 Corinthians 12:9).

Sister, no one wants pain or weakness, and we certainly don't want our struggles to be a detriment to our children. But maybe the cracks that we see as a hindrance to being the mom we want to be are actually the cracks God will use to enrich our children's lives with his wisdom, strength, and truth.

So pray that one day, in glory in your resurrected body, you will be able to look back and rejoice that the seeds of God's truth planted in your children's lives were watered every day as a result of God's grace pouring through the unwanted cracks in your earthly body. God has always worked through weakness. May he use yours to the end that little lives become resplendent with an array of the beautiful wild flowers of Christ's character and glory.

REFLECT

- ~ Do you see your weakness, illness, or limitations as a hindrance to your children?

- ~ What difference does it make (or would it make) for you to believe that God has allowed these cracks in your life and that he can redeem them for his purposes?

- ~ Can you see how God has used those same cracks to grow you and your children in ways you wouldn't change?

Journal

TWENTY-SIX

Grace for Raising a Strong-Willed Child

"As it is written: 'None is righteous, no, not one;
no one understands; no one seeks for God' ... But
now the righteousness of God has been manifested
apart from the law."

ROMANS 3:10-11, 21

GRACE IN A LINE

God is giving me everything I need to
parent the children he's given me.

My first child was born with a sweet temperament. He was a joy to parent! When we said no to something he shouldn't touch, his little lip would pucker up, and he would walk away without a fight. He slept through the night early, he was full of smiles, and he loved being with other people. I naively (and proudly) wondered deep down why other parents couldn't manage their children as well as I could. And then God humbled me by giving me a couple of strong-willed children, who liked to test the limits and were not afraid to put up a fight.

It took me a while, but I eventually came to see that each child, both the compliant and the strong-willed, was a gift from God's hand, given to bless us and for us to raise for his glory. Having said that, our stronger-willed children often required extra grace to parent when their little wills seemed bent toward defiance.

NO ONE IS TOO GOOD TO NEED GRACE

My purpose here is not to give strategies for raising a strong-willed child. There are other helpful resources available for that. (To name just two, Cynthia Tobias's books on this subject not only give helpful parenting strategies but point out the potential strengths of children with stronger temperaments. James Dobson has updated his book *The Strong-Willed Child*, which has served many parents over the years.) What I would like to do is to offer encouragement for you if you are raising children who see rules more as suggestions and boundaries as lines to be pushed.

First, remember that we are all rebels by nature—including you. We know this, but we so easily forget it. "None is righteous … no one seeks for God … no one does good, not even one" (Romans 3:10-12). We can look obedient outwardly while rebelling in our hearts. Compliant children might appear less sinful, but they may be people-pleasers who obey to get the praise of man rather than God or proud law-keepers who think God loves them because of their own goodness. Strong-willed children are less prone to hiding their rebellion, and so, while they may create more obvious parenting challenges, you rarely have to guess what's going on in their hearts. The point is that sin is sin, that no one obeys God's law, and that the only way to be righteous is to accept the gift of forgiveness that God offers in Christ. Kids with both kinds of temperament need to receive a new heart that loves and fears God and submits to his authority. All of us need Jesus to save us from ourselves.

Second, accept that parenting a child with a strong will is going to test us in certain ways. It can also expose sin in our own hearts, in those moments when we react wrongly to our child's sin. There is a danger that if we become overly focused on our child's disobedience, we might fail to see (or tend to excuse) what comes out of our own hearts in response. Impatience, anger, harsh discipline, hurtful words, and other ungodly reactions not only displease God but may plant the fear in our children that Jesus wouldn't want to save them because they are so bad and beyond hope. Remember that God graciously offers abundant forgiveness to both parents and children when we confess and repent of our sin against him. Although we cannot change our children's hearts, as we learn to rely on God's word for wisdom and pray for parenting grace each day, we can trust God to be faithful.

FIVE THINGS TO REMEMBER

Before I continue, let me mention something I've come to understand as a result of our own journey. While many children are born with a more naturally defiant nature, there are others that have physical and/or neurological challenges at play that may give the appearance of bad behavior and defiance, when in reality the truth is far more complex. Although sin always plays a role, children who deal with more complex challenges may require wisdom from outside resources. Sarah often felt shame and guilt over her child's behavior until she found out that he was battling an illness which affected his brain and therefore his ability to control himself. We need both to prayerfully seek wisdom from the Lord and be willing to turn to outside expert help for more extreme challenges.

For the majority, however, as you parent the children entrusted to you, let me encourage you with a few reminders that have strengthened me through the years.

Trust that God has created your children to be unique and given them to you to raise for his glory. There may be days when you don't feel that you have what it takes to be the parent of a particular child. (And if you do today, you might not tomorrow!) The truth is that, apart from God's help, none of us has what it takes to be a godly mom. But, as a mother who has fallen short in many ways, I can bear witness to God's faithfulness. As you look to him to equip and empower you, he will enable you to be the parent that your children need you to be.

Recognize that, whether your child is more compliant by nature or tests every limit, you need God's wisdom and God's work to raise children who love and obey Christ. "By wisdom a house is built, and by understanding it is established" (Proverbs 24:3). In both the seemingly easier seasons and the more difficult ones, God invites us to depend on him through prayer and daily meditating on his word. There is greater wisdom to be found there than in our own counsel. And as we look to him, he promises to guide our steps and give us grace upon grace for each of our children.

Strive to establish and communicate clear and realistic boundaries, along with the consequences a child will bear for disobedience. Along the way, I learned that wisdom looks like employing discipline that fits the crime whenever possible, giving consequences that we are willing (and able) to follow through with. It's also important to remember that different children will require different kinds of consequences. Giving one son a time-out in his room was not very effective because he was a reader and happily spent that time in a good book. Yet for our other, people-loving son, time away from the family was tantamount to solitary confinement.

Use every opportunity to model, teach, and apply gospel truth. Our children need to understand that we all come into the world as enemies of God and that there are eternal consequences for sin (Ephesians 2:1-3; Romans 6:23). As parents, it is our privilege to tell our children how they can be rescued from God's eternal wrath through God's Son, Jesus, and it is our duty to tell them that they need to be rescued. We can teach them that Jesus lived the perfect life of obedience that's impossible for them (and us), that he bore the penalty they (and we) deserve for rebelling against God, and that we can therefore repent and receive a new heart. And we can encourage them with the truth that, through God's word and his Holy Spirit, they can grow to obey and delight in God, serving him instead of their sinful desires. Strong-willed children give their parents plenty of opportunities to remind their children of these truths and help them apply them to their hearts and lives!

Guard your own heart. This is a particular word of warning to the parent who is by nature a rule-follower and is parenting a non-compliant child. Due to my personal record of "behavioral morality," I was much more challenged when parenting children who liked to test every boundary. My own high moral standards blinded me to my sins of pride, self-righteousness, and a critical spirit towards those who didn't follow the rules. I am deeply grateful for the way God used my strong-willed children to humble and sanctify me, even as he used me to help them (slowly) learn the goodness of loving authority in our lives. As he gently reminded me of the grace I had been given, he also taught me how to show grace towards my children, even when they needed discipline for disobedience.

In his wisdom, God has blessed you with each one of the children you have been given. He knows you will need him to be the mother they need, and when you look to him, you can be confident that he will be the Father you need to bring glory to him.

REFLECT

- ~ How does the truth that each of your children (compliant or strong-willed) comes into your family as a sinner lead you to prayerful dependence on God?

- ~ As you recognize both your need and the need of your children for God's mercy and grace, how does God's promise to provide all you need to parent encourage you today?

Journal

TWENTY - SEVEN

Grace for the Prodigal

*"When he came to himself, he said …
'I will arise and go to my father.'"*

LUKE 15:17-18

GRACE IN A LINE

*God can call wandering children back to him.
There is always hope.*

Linda

I walked behind the nurse as she led my daughter to a room stripped of everything but bare walls. The last thing I remember is the look of horror on Sarah's face when she realized she was being locked into a padded room until doctors were sure she would not harm herself.

As we drove away from our local mental facility, tears streamed down my face. This was the climax of many years of struggle between my 17-year-old daughter and me and, even more, between Sarah and the Lord. We had prayed, shed many tears, tried to reason with Sarah, and sought wisdom from others, but a frightening decision Sarah had made had led us to where we now were. As I poured out my fears and grief to the Lord on the car ride home, I surrendered her to my heavenly Father, and immediately felt that peace that really does transcend understanding wash over my soul.

Our troubles had begun during the middle-school years when Sarah found herself in a battle between the fear of man and the fear of God. Popularity was an alluring god, but she had grown up in a Christian home, and the truth rang in her ears. She felt under pressure to conform to the sexualized and godless culture that confronted her each day. The older she got, the harder she pushed against us and our boundaries, and the more distant we became. My husband and I found our only solace in prayer. Boldly I asked God to deliver the daughter I loved from her strong enemy, as David prayed in Psalm 18:6, 16:

> *"In my distress I called upon the LORD; to my God I cried for help … He sent from on high; he took me; he drew me out of many waters. He rescued me from my strong enemy and from those who hated me, for they were too mighty for me. They confronted me in the day of my calamity, but the LORD was my support. He brought me out into a broad place; he rescued me, because he delighted in me."*

God would hear our prayers for Sarah, but there was work he wanted to do in my life as well. As I spent increasing amounts of time in his word, God began to open my eyes to my own sin, particularly a spirit of self-righteousness that I had been blind to. As a born rule-follower I had struggled to relate to Sarah's hardness of heart. Then I began to understand that she viewed our biblical standards as impossible to meet while at the same time living in the world she found herself in. In my pride, I lacked the compassion and grace she needed when she was feeling lost, confused, and alone. It was through my own sense of helplessness and pain, when I felt like an utter failure as a mom, that God began a new work of humility and brokenness in me. Tearfully, I prayed and lamented my own sin, even while praying God's word on behalf of Sarah. And although on that dark day at the mental facility it felt as though the enemy had won a victory, in fact, as we were soon to see, it was all part of God's answer to those prayers.

Sarah

I squeezed my eyes shut, desperately hoping to find this was all just a horrible nightmare. But as I opened my eyes, the stark white walls and the ache in my gut jolted me into reality. This was a nightmare, but one I was very much living.

I was ashamed of who I'd become, angry at those who had hurt me along the way, and terrified of what was to come. But more than anything, I felt the weight of the world crashing down. I was in a pit so deep that I couldn't see the light. I was hurting, lost, and feeling hopeless. I had been raised to follow Christ, and for most of my childhood I had genuinely wanted to follow him, but the pressures and weight of the world had a grip around my neck, and I was tired of the battle. So. Unbelievably. Tired.

I glanced over at the Bible on my bed, the only thing the nurses would allow me to have, and I cracked it open. "God," I whispered, "I can't do this anymore. I don't know a way out of this pit, but if you're truly who you say you are, I need you to rescue me. I'm so sorry for trying to live my own way.

I know I don't deserve anything, but please, forgive me and give me the strength to go on."

Something strange washed over me. Was it... hope? Despite how much I was hurting, somehow I knew I was still loved. By God and by my parents. And in those moments, the oddest thing happened—the anger I had felt toward my parents, and especially my mom, for so long, began to dissipate. I had taken my hurt and anger out on my mom, knowing she was the only safe place. But I knew I would be welcomed home. I heard the words she had said to me: "No matter how much you push me away, I will always fight for you. Even if you can't see and believe the truth, I will believe enough for the both of us." My mom wasn't my enemy—she was simply the one the enemy had used to convince me that I could never live up to who God wanted me to be.

By God's grace, he rescued me from the pit of despair during my time in that pediatric psychiatric ward. I got there by trying to take my life, and I left there with a life worth living in Christ. And I know without a doubt that my parent's fervent prayers and unwillingness to give up fighting for me was a large part of what God used to draw me to him in my darkest hour. My mom—whom I had frequently told that I hated and never wanted to be like—is my dearest friend and sister in Christ. What the enemy meant for evil, the Lord has used for his good purposes. For, just as my mom prayed, he redeemed my life from the pit.

DON'T GIVE UP

Sister, if you have a child who is wandering from you and pushing against every boundary, or who is estranged, or who is rejecting Christ, I implore you—don't give up. If they still have breath, they—and you—still have hope. And I want to encourage you to fight with these three tools that can be gleaned from the story of the prodigal son in Luke 15...

1. *Patience:* Patience to keep asking questions, keep listening, keep trying, keep seeking to understand. Resist the temptation to try to coerce or emotionally manipulate your child into returning spiritually. The father in the story of the prodigal son let his son leave and go to the distant country. And then he waited and watched.

Most likely, your child's choices stem from many complexities. Although sin is always involved, there can also be hurt, fear, insecurity, self-protection, shame, and countless other elements contributing to their decisions. Understanding these will help you interact with greater compassion, wisdom, and patience as you wait and watch.

2. *Love:* The father never stopped loving. He was always looking for his son's return, and he was ready to run down the road: "But while he was a still a long way off, his father saw him and felt compassion, and ran and embraced him and kissed him" (Luke 15:20). In that society, to run in that way was to do something shameful. That did not stop this father. Love sped him down that road. God is like that to your child. And you can mirror that to your child with the Lord's strength.

3. *Hope:* The son in the story needed to leave in order to understand how much he needed his father and to understand the love of his father. Pray for your child's heart, and don't give up. I remember my mom saying that she prayed that God would allow whatever I needed in order to draw my heart to him and save me from the world and myself. That was a scary prayer to pray, and she never could have imagined

the scary way in which God was going to answer that prayer. But he did answer it. We don't have a guarantee of our child's salvation or every prodigal's return, but we can always pray to that end and trust that God hears us. Don't lose hope. God is a God of miracles and redemption, regardless of how dark things may seem. Pray that this proves to be the path that leads to the place where your child can come to know God as Father.

In his grace, God never let me go, as hard as I ran. In his grace, he used that season to rescue me and to change my mom. And I'm praying that, in his grace, God will bring your child back too—back to his loving embrace and his heavenly home.

REFLECT

- Do you have a wandering or rebellious child who keeps you up at night with worry and fear, or maybe even anger and frustration?

- How might God want to use your child's struggles to do a new work in your own heart?

- How does the parable of the prodigal son and our own mother-daughter journey give you hope?

Journal

TWENTY-EIGHT

How Grace Defeats the Joy-Stealer of Comparison

"For as in one body we have many members, and the members do not all have the same function, so we, though many, are one body in Christ, and individually members one of another. Having gifts that differ according to the grace given to us, let us use them."

ROMANS 12:4-6

GRACE IN A LINE

God loves me! I really don't need to seek reassurance by comparing myself with other moms.

The early 20th-century US president Theodore Roosevelt once said, "Comparison is the thief of joy."

And for moms, the comparison trap seems to be around every corner:

- *It's so unfair that she has had multiple children and doesn't even seem to appreciate them, while I've endured miscarriages and difficulty in conceiving.*

- *Look at that mom's house. It's always so put together, while mine constantly looks like an atomic bomb hit it. Why can't I be more be organized like her?*

- *I can't believe that mom went back to work right after having her child. It would be so much better for her kids if she stayed home with them like I did.*

- *She's in amazing shape after having four children. I'm so embarrassed by how my body looks even years after giving birth.*

- *Those children are so disrespectful. I'm so glad my kids don't act like that.*

- *Her son got into a prestigious college and mine barely survived high school. I wish my child was more motivated, like hers.*

Can you relate? Once you realize how you're tempted to compare yourself to others, you notice it all the time. And maybe you notice that it never makes you feel more joyful or more godly—it only makes you feel prouder or more insecure. That's because these are what almost always lie at the root of our comparing ourselves with others—insecurity or pride.

INSECURITY
There's no exact formula for motherhood (aside from what Scripture calls us to do as followers of Christ and examples to our children), and we have to make endless choices that have no black-and-white answer. Not only does that lead us to second-guess every decision we make, but it fans the flame of insecurity every time we see another mom living out her role differently than we are.

Social media, despite the many wonderful things about it, tends to foster this insecurity. As I scroll through my social-media feed, I will inevitably come across a mom sharing something about how she makes her home a structured, well-oiled machine. And as I look around at my home… well, let's just say a structured, well-oiled machine it is not.

If I'm not careful, that one post can create a joy-sucking inner monologue that says, "My house isn't as organized as hers because I'm just not working hard enough. If only I was more like her, this house would look so much better. And maybe my children would be better behaved too. I bet my children would be better off with a healthy mom like her."

Is this woman wrong for sharing her tips? Not necessarily (although at times it may be helpful to include caveats reminding us that the tips may not be realistic for all people). No—the issue lies primarily in my own heart, not in her feed, because at that moment, I'm comparing the inside of my life with the outward appearance of hers, and I'm basing my own sense of self-worth on how I measure up against her.

If there were any doubt that the issue is in my own heart, it's made even clearer by what tends to happen next—the way that very quickly I try to settle my own insecurities by criticizing this woman, whom I've never even met: "She probably thinks she knows everything. She probably has no idea what it's like to have circumstances like mine. I bet she has it so easy. She's not as perfect as she thinks."

These ugly thoughts are hard to admit to on paper, but the sin underneath each one lies within each of our hearts (Jeremiah 17:9). It's a refusal to find our sense of self and our sense of contentment in knowing and being loved by Jesus. So we either desire a life God hasn't given us or we tear down others in our hearts because their successes or blessings make us feel the sting of our own weaknesses, shortcomings, or circumstances.

None of that makes us feel better. It only sends us spiraling further into discontentment, shame and loneliness, and greater insecurity.

PRIDE

On the other hand, we can find ourselves slipping into a pattern of pride when we compare ourselves with others and measure up well. We see a mom walking by us in the grocery store with a child throwing a tantrum, and we think, "Wow, she's clearly not disciplining and teaching her children like she should be. I'm so glad my kids don't act like that." Or we're a stay-at-home mom, and we pat ourselves on the back because we've done the more "honorable" thing than being a working mom. Or vice versa. Or we homeschool, and deep down we think that anyone who chooses public (state) school is foolish for giving their child's education to someone else (or, again, vice versa).

In doing this, we're looking to our own perceived successes to justify and validate ourselves. We want to feel that we're doing a great job, and we do this by looking down on others. The problem is that it's ugly, when we stop and think about it. Instead of loving a struggling mom and pausing to pray for her or thinking of how we could help her, we're just using her as a tool to help ourselves feel good.

This, then, is the comparison trap. And it's easier to spot than it is to not step into it. But the good news is that there's a better way.

Grace.

With the help of the Holy Spirit, we have been given the tools we need to fight this comparison battle and embrace the joy God has for us, by receiving his grace and then offering it to others.

LIVING BY GRACE

I'm so thankful that God hasn't left us to ourselves. With Christ, we are equipped to fight with truth. The gospel tells us that it is "by grace you have been saved through faith. And this is not your own doing; it is the gift of God, not a result of works, so that no one can boast" (Ephesians 2:8-9).

We fight comparison by remembering that none of us have earned or deserve anything. All is a gift of God's grace through Jesus Christ.

Grace tells me that what I most need I didn't earn, so my performance can never gain what matters—leaving no room for pride.

Grace tells me that God is always near and giving me what I need: both eternal salvation and daily mercies. So God can and will use me despite, and even in, my weaknesses—so there's no need for insecurity.

DIFFERENT STORIES, EQUAL VALUE

Every mom has different circumstances, children, opportunities, challenges, strengths, weaknesses, and stories, which together mean we can play a unique role in the kingdom of God. Instead of seeing our differences (including mothering styles) as something to compare ourselves against, we can ask the Holy Spirit to help us change the narrative to see that those differences are from the hand of our heavenly Father, who has given each of us different roads to travel for his purposes—each road unique in circumstances but equal in value and given in grace.

Sister, seek to spend more time remembering the Lord's grace to you and asking for wisdom to mother your children than you do measuring how you stack up against the moms around you. Then you will increasingly experience the peace and joy of knowing that you are right where he wants you, and that he is right there with you; because the truth is that if we knew what he knows, we wouldn't want our life to be any other way.

Rest in that. And know that you are loved, not because of what you do or how you compare to the moms around you but because of whose you are. It's grace that sets you free from the joy-stealing trap of comparison.

REFLECT

- Can you relate to certain traps of comparison? Do you see areas where comparison tempts you toward insecurity or pride?

- What truths can you write down to refer to when comparison starts to steal your joy?

Journal

TWENTY-NINE

Enjoying the Little Things

*"Behold, what I have seen to be good and fitting is to eat
and drink and find enjoyment in all the toil with which
one toils under the sun the few days of his life that God
has given him, for this is his lot."*

ECCLESIASTES 5:18

GRACE IN A LINE

Moments of joy are gifts from God for me
to notice, pause in, and enjoy.

*"Mom, remember when we had a 'no manners' night at
the dinner table? Remember when dad threw his food
into the air and tried to catch it in his mouth by diving
off of his chair? That was the best! I still laugh every time
I think about it!"*

Yep—out of all our deep conversations, devotional times,
and teachable moments, this is the sort of memory that
sticks out for my kids.

Why?!

It's because there's something about laughing and being lighthearted with our kids that connects us in a unique way. We're not just being their mom; we're enjoying being their mom. And they remember that.

I know how easy it is to get caught up in the seriousness and weightiness and sheer busyness of motherhood. But there's a risk that we sometimes forget to enjoy the simple pleasures of parenting life—the laughter, goofiness, and fun. And when I hear my children remind me of a memory like this with beaming smiles, it often cuts through the thick cloud of burdens and concerns, and reminds me that it's okay for motherhood to be fun too, even in more difficult seasons. And it reminds me that we have to have the eyes to see it and the willingness to embrace it.

DON'T FORGET TO LAUGH!

Even when (especially when) motherhood feels hard and life feels heavy, moments of laughter are truly gifts from God. They help us retain a sense of childlike wonder. They help us build relationships with our children in a way that shows we simply enjoy them and want them to enjoy us. And if we stop to look, there are little moments like this around every corner. Whether it's stopping to laugh at your child's joke, which made so little sense that it was actually hilarious, or having a spontaneous dance party even when you have two left feet, it will always be worth it.

No matter what season of life you are in with your kids, it's a gift to laugh with your children and find ways to bring lighthearted moments in. Not only are your own spirits lifted, but your children learn that they can have joy and laughter because this life is a good gift from God, even when it's hard—that we are meant to enjoy life as God created us to!

As King Solomon learned as he searched for the purpose in all his toil "under the sun":

> *"Behold, what I have seen to be good and fitting is to eat and drink and find enjoyment in all the toil with which one toils under the sun the few days of his life that God has given him, for this is his lot." (Ecclesiastes 5:18)*

While that might sound somewhat fatalistic, there is truth in the fact that, although we will toil all the days of our life, including the long and hard days of our motherhood, it is good and right to enjoy the gifts God has given us. And one of those many gifts is our children.

I don't say this to add another burden to your already long list of things to do as a mom: "I must make time to laugh with my kids. I must make time to make memories. I have 15 minutes after cooking dinner and before football pick-up. I'll schedule it in for then." No—this is permission to bask in God's grace over you and to embrace the beauty and joy of motherhood in all the little moments around you.

What might change if you took the time to set aside your burdens and to-do lists for a few moments today, knowing the Lord will equip you for all of it when the time comes, and give yourself permission to take some time with your kids to laugh, be lighthearted, and simply enjoy them? Maybe you could…

- ~ have a no-silverware dinner night when you can just embrace the mess of everyone using their hands instead. (Yes, this may be very hard for those of you who have a high need for cleanliness!)

- watch (and do) an exercise video with your children and let them laugh hysterically as you fall over trying to do an awkward stretch or get into a challenging pose.

- try to make up your own jokes with your kids and see who can come up with the best one.

- have a family game night.

- put a pause on meal prep and dance in the kitchen when your child grabs your hand as music plays in the background.

- put that dirty bouquet of dandelion weeds you've just been handed in a little jar as if it's as beautiful as a bouquet of roses and put it as a centerpiece on the counter.

- go down the slide at the park with your children, even though you get stuck halfway or it makes your hair stand on end.

- belt out a familiar song with your kids, even if you can't hold a tune.

- show your children what not to do when it comes to manners at the dinner table. They will probably learn their manners better by watching you break all the "manners rules" in a humorous way than if you simply tell them over and over the right rules!

The list could go on, and what that list might look like will be different for each of us depending on our circumstances, children, and personalities. But the point is this: it's all too easy to forget to enjoy our children and embrace moments of fun and laughter because they don't feel as important as the serious conversations, the needed discipline, or the many things we have to get done. But God wants us to truly enjoy the journey of motherhood and to build relationships with our children because he is a Father full of joy, and he desires a relationship with us in which we can know him and enjoy him—not just fear him.

BLESSING-COUNTING MATTERS MORE THAN SOCK-SORTING

So sister, take a deep breath, set aside your many swirling thoughts, and take a moment to count the many blessings you have as a mom. It doesn't really matter if the socks don't get sorted, or your work gets done a little more hurriedly this week, or the house is a mess when you go to bed. Ask the Lord to renew in you a sense of joy and give you eyes to see moments when you can pause, put down your chores, embrace the moment at hand, and simply enjoy your children.

Yes, motherhood is hard, and motherhood is weighty. But it is also filled with countless treasures to be found and enjoyed as you raise precious lives for the short time they have been entrusted to you. So, don't miss those. Because it's those little moments—of joy, laughter, and sweet relationship—that will stand out in your children's minds as memories that are worth remembering forever.

REFLECT

- ~ What are a few memories that bring a smile to your mind as you think of your children? Thank God for those moments!

- ~ If you are in a season that feels heavy or more taxing, what are some manageable ways you can make room for moments to simply enjoy your children? Ask God for the eyes to see and the ability to embrace these moments when they come.

Journal

THIRTY

Daily Grace for Real Moms

"But if it is by grace, it is no longer on the basis of works; otherwise grace would no longer be grace."

ROMANS 11:6

GRACE IN A LINE

I will always need grace, and God will always give me grace.

It was a warm spring day, and our boys had a couple of friends over to play. While they were outside, I decided to bake a batch of large chocolate-chip cookies to make ice-cream sandwiches for a family treat later that day. Taking them out of the oven, I left the cookies cooling on a rack while I went to put in another load of laundry. Fifteen minutes later I walked into the kitchen and stared in disbelief. Where there had once been a dozen cookies cooling, now there was only one.

I ran outside and began reprimanding the boys for eating the cookies without asking permission. All four children insisted on their innocence, but I knew they were guilty, and so I warned them of the even greater sin of lying about what they had done.

Several hours later our six-month-old Labrador puppy began throwing up chocolate.

I realized that I had completely misjudged the situation. Thankfully, after I had humbly asked the boys to forgive me, we all laughed about it in the end. But it was another reminder that real moms need God's grace every single day.

The cookie debacle was not the first (or last) time that I would make an incorrect judgment when it came to my children. While I did my best to arbitrate justice in the heat of siblings arguing, resolve neighborhood squabbles, or discern whether a child was being honest, I often fell short of getting things right. God alone sees and knows the hearts of our children and the circumstances he uses to grow them (and us!). We are not God, and so we won't always get our judgment calls right when it comes to our kids.

And actually, we are not always right when we make judgment calls about ourselves, either. Moms are particularly great at being hard on ourselves and deciding that we're falling short in all kinds of ways:...

- When it seems that other moms are more creative or fun than we are, we can question what we have to offer our kids.

- When we struggle to connect and communicate with our teenager who seems to talk so easily with others, it can convince us that we're not capable of loving our teen well.

- When chronic pain or a long illness limits us from being fully present or able to do what we'd like with our children, we can feel discouraged.

~ When one of our kids has special needs that require a disproportionate amount of time and attention, we can feel guilty for having less to give to our other children.

Sometimes we ask more of ourselves than God does. We put pressure on ourselves to be "Supermom" when God knows we are dependent creatures, who can do nothing apart from him, (John 15:5). Knowing (and remembering) that God loves us and loves our kids liberates us from thinking we need to be it all or do it all. On the other hand, there are (many) times when we are right to feel guilty because we really have fallen short of what God calls for—and then there is grace for us in the gospel. At the cross, we are forgiven and given a clean slate, and can move forward with joy and confidence in God, who loves to lavish his children with grace.

Romans 11:6 reminds us that neither our salvation nor our lives as believers is ever about works. It's never about what we do, what we achieve, or how well we mother. From beginning to end, from first to last, it's always and only about God's grace.

Consider these ways in which God offers real grace to weak, inadequate, and imperfect moms who run to him.

~ When you feel weak and weary, you can find renewed strength in Christ and put God's glory on display. It's helpful to remind ourselves regularly that we live in an unfair world, we are raising little sinners, and we lack what it takes to raise God-glorifying children apart from God's grace and truth. As we confess our need for him and lean upon his strength, we will find courage and confidence in knowing that God can use even our failures redemptively.

~ When you feel inadequate and insufficient as a parent, you can find hope in the perfect sufficiency of God. Though we tend to misjudge other people, situations, and even our own hearts, God is the perfect judge. He sees all things, and he is providentially and wisely guiding and sanctifying us as we parent in the hope of the gospel.

~ When you recognize that you will always fall short, you can bear witness to the hope of the gospel. God's Son, Jesus, lived a perfect life on our behalf, suffered, and died on a cross to save sinners. As those who have been redeemed, we can rest in the promise that "there is … no condemnation for those who are in Christ" (Romans 8:1). God draws near to the humble and contrite in spirit. So let your weakness lead you to your gracious Savior, and let it show others in your household and neighborhood what it means to know that you're a sinner but know too that you're forgiven.

~ When you are tempted to compare yourself to other moms, remember that God uniquely designed you to parent the children he has given you to raise. You might be the super-fun mom—or you might not. You might be able to juggle homeschooling with keeping an organized home and cooking meals everyone loves—or you might not. While we should always strive to be and do our best, God has given us each different gifts and varying circumstances, and he calls us to live faithfully and contentedly, serving him exactly where he has planted us for his glory.

~ When you lack wisdom and insight to raise godly children in this fallen world, you can run to the all-knowing, wise, and sovereign God. God is light, and nothing is hidden from him (Luke 12:2-3). True wisdom is trusting that God sees and knows all and that he is able to equip us to do all that he calls us to do (Hebrews 13:20-21).

God's grace is for real moms. There is sweet relief in acknowledging that, while God calls each of us to a life of holiness, he is fully committed to conforming us to the image of his Son as we put our hope in him and depend on his word and Spirit (Philippians 1:6), and he is equally committed to forgiving us for all our failings as we walk by faith in his Son. You will not reach perfection until you get to heaven, but you can strive to walk according to the grace given to you through the gospel. Your children do not need a perfect mother. What they do need is a mother who recognizes her need for a perfect Savior, and understands that that is the greatest need of her children as well—a mother who knows that she has a Father who always, always gives more grace.

Sister, today, may you find rest in this life-giving truth as you navigate the countless ups and downs of motherhood. You will fall short. You will not always get it right. And you will love your children with an imperfect love. But your heavenly Father sees you and knows exactly what you need to be the mother of your precious children.

Motherhood may be filled with many unknowns, but you can find confidence and assurance in this…

He gives more grace.

REFLECT

- How does understanding your own constant need for grace protect you from either becoming self-righteous or beating yourself up when you feel like a failure?

- How does understanding God's extravagant grace encourage you in the midst of your sin and weakness and also give you more compassion for your children when they sin?

- How does a greater understanding of God's grace for you in motherhood offer you encouragement, hope, and help moving forward?

Journal

Acknowledgments

Although our names may be on the cover of this book, we are far from the only ones who have made it what it is. First and foremost, we thank our Lord and Savior, Jesus Christ. The words on the pages of this book have come out of the overflow of the forgiveness, love, and grace we have received through the cross and his sanctifying work in our life.

Thank you to our husbands, Ray and Jeff, for your unceasing support, love, and encouragement through this journey of motherhood, as well as through the writing process. Thank you for being our faithful partners in life and parenthood, men of integrity, and godly examples to our children.

Linda: To my adult children Michael, Stephen, and Sarah, who have been God's instruments in my journey of growing in the grace of Jesus Christ. I thank the Lord for the godly character that each of you demonstrate in your work and homes. And, while my primary role as your mother is long past, I continue to pray that, by God's grace, you will love the Lord with all of your heart and with all your soul and with all your mind (Matthew 22:37). I have no greater joy than to hear that my children are walking in the truth (3 John 4). Wherever God leads you in your own journey of parenting and life, always remember that he gives more grace.

Sarah: To my children, Ben, Hannah, Haley, and Eli. I'm a far cry from the mom I want to be, but I thank you for your patience and grace with me as I strive with the strength of God to be a mom who loves and leads you well. I'm so thankful for your unique personalities and strengths, your tenacity through the many challenges you've faced, and the way you bring untold joy into my life. I pray with every ounce of my being that you will come to know and experience the love of Jesus in a way that will shape you into men and women of godly character—not because you're good enough, but because his grace is.

To Carl, our unsung hero. You are not only a phenomenal editor and wise counselor, you are a dear friend and brother in Christ. Thank you for your incredible ability to shape our writing in a way that brings out the best in us while always doing so with grace, sensitivity, and a healthy dose of British humor. We are incredibly grateful for you.

And lastly, thank you to the many friends and family who have been an integral part of our lives, spurring us on, praying for us, encouraging us, and leading by example. You have left more of an impact on our lives than you will ever know.

thegoodbook
COMPANY

BIBLICAL | RELEVANT | ACCESSIBLE

At The Good Book Company, we are dedicated to helping Christians and local churches grow. We believe that God's growth process always starts with hearing clearly what he has said to us through his timeless word—the Bible.

Ever since we opened our doors in 1991, we have been striving to produce Bible-based resources that bring glory to God. We have grown to become an international provider of user-friendly resources to the Christian community, with believers of all backgrounds and denominations using our books, Bible studies, devotionals, evangelistic resources, and DVD-based courses.

We want to equip ordinary Christians to live for Christ day by day, and churches to grow in their knowledge of God, their love for one another, and the effectiveness of their outreach.

Call us for a discussion of your needs or visit one of our local websites for more information on the resources and services we provide.

Your friends at The Good Book Company

thegoodbook.com | thegoodbook.co.uk
thegoodbook.com.au | thegoodbook.co.nz
thegoodbook.co.in